OX   ΓS

Series Editor: Steven Croft

Thomas Middleton

The Revenger's Tragedy

Edited by Jackie Moore

Oxford University Press

OXFORD
UNIVERSITY PRESS

Great Clarendon Street, Oxford OX2 6DP

Oxford University Press is a department of the University of Oxford.
It furthers the University's objective of excellence in research, scholarship,
and education by publishing worldwide in

Oxford   New York

Auckland   Cape Town   Dar es Salaam   Hong Kong   Karachi
Kuala Lumpur   Madrid   Melbourne   Mexico City   Nairobi
New Delhi   Shanghai   Taipei   Toronto

With offices in

Argentina   Austria   Brazil   Chile   Czech Republic   France   Greece
Guatemala   Hungary   Italy   Japan   South Korea   Poland   Portugal
Singapore   Switzerland   Thailand   Turkey   Ukraine   Vietnam

Oxford is a registered trade mark of Oxford University Press
in the UK and in certain other countries

British Library Cataloguing in Publication Data

Data available

ISBN: 978-0-19-912954-6

1 3 5 7 9 10 8 6 4 2

Typeset in India by TNQ Books and Journals Pvt. Ltd.

Printed by Printplus, China

Paper used in the production of this book is a natural, recyclable product made from
wood grown in sustainable forests. The manufacturing process conforms to the
environmental regulations of the country of origin.

The publishers would like to thank the following for permission to reproduce
photographs:

Page 4: The College of Arms; page 7: The Folger Shakespeare Library; page 19: The
President and Fellows of Magdalen College, Oxford; pages 155 and 170: Alex Cox; page
183: Bibliotheek der Rijksuniversiteit, Utrecht; page 207: National Portrait Gallery,
London; page 221: Jonathan Oakes/Royal Exchange Theatre
Illustrations Page 11: David Seaver; page 14: Martin Cottam

Contents

Acknowledgements

The text of the play is taken from *Four Revenge Tragedies*, edited by Katharine Eisaman Maus (Oxford World's Classics, 1998).

The extract from the *Authorized Version of the Bible* (*The King James Bible*), the rights in which are vested in the Crown, is reproduced by permission of the Crown's Patentee, Cambridge University Press.

Acknowledgements from Jackie Moore

I would like to thank Steven Croft for his unfailing support and guidance. I am very grateful to Jan Doorly for her sensitive and scholarly editing and her sound judgement. I am indebted to my friend and colleague Paul Dean for his help in my research and for our valuable discussions, and I would like to pay tribute to a late colleague, Chris Jordan, who shared my passion for Middleton's writing. Finally, I would like to thank all at OUP who have helped bring this project to fruition.

Editors

Steven Croft, the series editor, holds degrees from Leeds and Sheffield universities. He has taught at secondary and tertiary level and headed the Department of English and Humanities in a tertiary college. He has 25 years' examining experience at A level and is currently a Principal Examiner for English. He has written several books on teaching English at A level, and his publications for Oxford University Press include *Exploring Literature*, *Success in AQA Language and Literature* and *Exploring Language and Literature*.

Jackie Moore read English Language and Literature at the University of Manchester with Elizabethan and Jacobean drama as a special option. She was later awarded her doctorate in English Literature with Philosophy. After lecturing in literature in higher education, she moved to the secondary sector, becoming head of an English department. She is now an educational consultant and Senior Examiner in English Literature for national and international examinations, and is the author of several books on A level literature.

Foreword

Oxford Student Texts, under the founding editorship of Victor Lee, have established a reputation for presenting literary texts to students in both a scholarly and an accessible way. The new editions aim to build on this successful approach. They have been written to help students, particularly those studying English literature for AS or A level, to develop an increased understanding of their texts. Each volume in the series, which covers a selection of key poetry and drama texts, consists of four main sections which link together to provide an integrated approach to the study of the text.

The first part provides important background information about the writer, his or her times and the factors that played an important part in shaping the work. This discussion sets the work in context and explores some key contextual factors.

This section is followed by the poetry or play itself. The text is presented without accompanying notes so that students can engage with it on their own terms without the influence of secondary ideas. To encourage this approach, the Notes are placed in the third section, immediately following the text. The Notes provide explanations of particular words, phrases, images, allusions and so forth, to help students gain a full understanding of the text. They also raise questions or highlight particular issues or ideas which are important to consider when arriving at interpretations.

The fourth section, Interpretations, goes on to discuss a range of issues in more detail. This involves an examination of the influence of contextual factors as well as looking at such aspects as language and style, and various critical views or interpretations. A range of activities for students to carry out, together with discussions as to how these might be approached, are integrated into this section.

At the end of each volume there is a selection of Essay Questions, a Chronology, and a Further Reading list.

We hope you enjoy reading this text and working with these supporting materials, and wish you every success in your studies.

Steven Croft   *Series Editor*

Thomas Middleton in Context

The authorship of *The Revenger's Tragedy*

In 1607 the population of London exceeded 200,000 inhabitants, swollen by those from the provinces who saw the city as a land of promise where the quality of life might be improved and fortunes made. Thousands of European and international immigrants moved in, literally tinkers, tailors, soldiers, sailors and spies. Others brought their skills in the arts, in crafts and trades, and in matters of finance that could be useful in the great economic boom taking place in England. London had a heady, cosmopolitan air.

King James I had succeeded to the throne in 1603, and already scandalous rumours of his self-indulgence and excess were circulating among his subjects. However, he was an educated and cultured king who was a patron of the arts, and was especially supportive of court theatre. This taste for the theatre was shared by his subjects.

The huge population needed diversions for their leisure hours, and London offered plenty; street entertainment was lively, including jugglers, acrobats, musicians, dancers and ballad singers. The Jacobeans (the name derives from *Jacobus*, the Latin version of James, the king's name) were not squeamish; they enjoyed watching public executions, especially when traitors were hanged, drawn and quartered, as were the Gunpowder Plotters of 1605. There was bull- and bear-baiting, cockfighting, the delights and dangers of drinking and gambling in the noisy taverns, and the bawdy pleasures of the many brothels. However, people also flocked to the most fashionable destination of all, the theatre.

There were at least six public, open-air playhouses, some capable of seating over 3,000 playgoers, and there were two smaller, more sophisticated indoor theatres seating up to a thousand. The public theatres played six days per week when possible, with the indoor theatres offering slightly fewer public performances. Playgoers would regularly attend more than one theatre, choosing the best and the newest productions; commercial theatre had been born and new material was constantly needed. Playwrights sometimes worked collaboratively, sometimes independently to feed this huge appetite. To help pay the massive costs of the new theatres and their companies, plays were written as quickly as possible and then handed over for the compulsory registration at the Stationers' Office. In such haste, errors were bound to occur.

So it happened with *The Revenger's Tragedy*, which was registered unsigned in 1607, along with *A Trick to Catch the Old One*, one copy of which was signed 'TM' for Thomas Middleton. Errors seemed to multiply in naming the author of *The Revenger's Tragedy*. Despite the contemporary convention that when two plays with a single author were handed in, both plays would be assigned to him, the author of this play remained anonymous until 1656, when a bookseller called Edward Archer attributed the play to Cyril Tourneur (1575–1626), the author of *The Atheist's Tragedy*. Francis Kirkman repeated this attribution in his 1661 and 1671 catalogues of plays and authors.

But there was a lingering uncertainty. There was external evidence suggesting that Thomas Middleton was indeed the author, such as Nathaniel Richards' commendatory verse for Middleton's *Women Beware Women*, which quotes from *The Revenger's Tragedy* in its second line (*drab of state*, IV.iv.72). As for internal evidence, it was recognized that there are striking similarities in character, language and situation between *The Revenger's Tragedy* and Middleton's other plays. But still doubt remained.

Stronger evidence first appeared in the preliminary but limited comparative studies of E.H.C. Oliphant in 1926. This work was confirmed with more certainty in the linguistic analyses of David J. Lake, MacDonald P. Jackson and R.V. Holdsworth (see Further Reading page 232). Holdsworth pointed to the fact that Edward

Archer had been wrong in half of his attributions. Work was carried out comparing over 700 plays, and it became clear that *The Revenger's Tragedy* revealed language and spelling that were unique to Middleton and evident across the body of his work. Further detailed computer analyses, such as that by M.W.A. Smith in 1991, have confirmed these findings. R.V. Holdsworth, after a lifetime's work in this area, is certain that Middleton is the author, and subsequent studies attribute the play to him. The Chadwyck-Healey electronic database *English Drama* put the case beyond reasonable doubt in establishing that Middleton's peculiarities of language were even rarer elsewhere than first thought. We can say with confidence that Thomas Middleton is the author of this wonderful play.

The life of Thomas Middleton

Thomas Middleton was born in 1580 into a prosperous family living in Old Jewry, next to wealthy Cheapside and St Paul's (see the map on page 11, which shows St Lawrence Jewry, where Middleton was baptized). His father William, a member of the Worshipful Company of Tilers and Bricklayers, was placed firmly within the urban middle class; he had been granted a coat of arms in 1568.

Middleton would have his first experience of the theatre while collecting rents for his father's tenements in Shoreditch adjoining the Curtain Theatre (see page 10), leased for 50 years. On the death of his father in 1586, his family's future seemed secure as the estate also included a 500-year lease on a house and wharf in Limehouse and copyhold on property in Hertfordshire.

But this financial security was quickly endangered by two reckless marriages. His mother Anne married an adventurer (Thomas Harvey, 20 years her junior) nine months after his father's death, and his sister Avis married a clothworker, Allan

Design for the Middleton coat of arms, granted to the playwright's father in 1568

Waterer, in 1598. In Elizabethan law a married woman could not own property but, guided by her late husband, Anne had set up a trust to protect the children's interests, and gave them one third each of the £100 bequeathed. Harvey, her new husband, seemed to accept this, but immediately after their marriage he began legal proceedings to acquire Anne's property. Although she fought hard against him, surviving an attempted poisoning for which he was imprisoned in 1595, Harvey sued again in 1600, and he finally acquired all the family property. He must have been furious to discover that the penniless Thomas Middleton had sold the Limehouse property to his sister's husband, Waterer, in 1599, and the rest of the property in 1600, to help him to finance his years of study.

Middleton's brother-in-law was sharp and his sister naïve; Waterer succeeded in acquiring his wife's property, and while living in his mother-in-law's home, he almost gained hers as well. Inevitably a series of legal and physical scraps between Harvey and Waterer followed, as they fought for the family property. Middleton was repeatedly called back from his studies in Oxford to intervene for his mother in a series of bitter lawsuits.

The entire sequence of events demonstrated that real life could be just as bizarre as that portrayed on stage. Such matters were soon echoed in Middleton's 'city comedies' such as *Michaelmas Term* (1604) and *A Trick to Catch the Old One* (1605), whose plots revolve around attempts to trick innocent young men out of their inheritance, an issue that is also relevant to *The Revenger's Tragedy*. However, Middleton's experiences were not unusual in a society that had become increasingly likely to pursue lawsuits.

As a young boy, Middleton must have been glad to escape the family disputes to attend his London grammar school, where he would have studied classical languages and literature; he became interested in certain European authors including the Italian political writer Niccolo Machiavelli (1469–1527) and the Spanish satirist Miguel de Cervantes (1547–1616); both influences would become evident in his own works. Middleton went as an undergraduate to Queen's College, Oxford where the curriculum included logic and rhetoric. Acting formed part of the study of rhetoric, and perhaps he played in the traditional Christmas Revels.

Middleton's struggle was typical of the educated but poor gentlemen represented by Vindice and Hippolito in *The Revenger's Tragedy*. Running out of money, he was forced to leave the university without a degree. He had attempted unsuccessfully to gain the patronage first of the Earl of Essex, to whom he dedicated his poem *The Wisdom of Solomon Paraphrased* in 1597, then of William, Second Baron Compton, to whom he dedicated another poem, *The Ghost of Lucrece*, in 1599. Although these poems were unsuccessful, the issue of violated chastity that he

5

took up in his early works would resurface in his later plays, such as with the character of Castiza in *The Revenger's Tragedy*.

Having published some satires and poetry, Middleton became an aspiring playwright, working with actors and their companies. His 1603 marriage to Mary Magdalen Marbeck would have influenced this decision: her brother was an actor with a prestigious company, the Admiral's Men, and her educated and cultured family was involved in the Church, law, and education.

Middleton's first paid commission was *Caesar's Fall*, a lost play for the Admiral's Men on which he collaborated in 1602 with Thomas Dekker, Michael Drayton, Anthony Munday and John Webster for a fee of £8 (an artisan's earnings at that time were between £11 and £14 per year). Middleton also wrote for several other acting companies, including the Children of Paul's and the King's Men. He found his material all around him; he was familiar with all aspects of London life, including the taverns populated by thieves, pickpockets, cutpurses and confidence tricksters. He saw the daily promenade at old St Paul's, and came into contact with the transient international population that was drawn to the great port of London.

Together with William Shakespeare (with whom he probably collaborated on *Timon of Athens* in about 1605) and Ben Jonson, he was considered one of the greatest of contemporary playwrights; he furthered his reputation by writing great masques for civic pageants. *The Revenger's Tragedy* was written in 1606, and he later wrote two other great tragedies, *Women Beware Women* in 1621, and *The Changeling* (with William Rowley) in 1622. Probably his greatest contemporary success was *A Game at Chess*, 1624, in which he drew on current hostility to Spain by satirizing the relationship between the Spanish and the British. But this was also his downfall, as the city authorities banned further performances of the play after the Spanish Ambassador complained to the king, and Middleton seems to have written little thereafter. His work for civic and royal pageants dried up, and the impoverished Draper's Society failed to pay for his last masque, *The Triumphs of Health and Prosperity*, in 1626. He died penniless in 1627.

An engraved portrait of Thomas Middleton published in 1657

Thomas Middleton seems to have been something of a loner. Unlike Shakespeare, he did not own shares in a theatre company; unlike Jonson, he did not publish his collected works. Much evidence of his collaborative work and the authorship of his plays has disappeared. But happily, in our own day his great talent as one of our leading writers is recognized and his true status is being revealed.

Middleton's society

Jacobean society should have been prosperous. James I had signed a peace treaty with Spain in 1604, ending years of mutual suspicion and anxiety; the port of London was one of the greatest in the world; there was an economic boom, and a widespread appreciation of the arts. But prosperity did not follow. Instead, under James's rule society suffered from extreme divisions between the rich and the poor, and the destruction of the support system that had existed under a traditional feudal society. The concepts and practices of the justice system were also weakened.

In the city and the countryside, the poor suffered dreadfully; 1594 saw the first of a series of bad harvests, which drove up the cost of basic foods such as bread. The population far exceeded the demand for labour in both agricultural and industrial work. But this was an extremely hierarchical society: at the top were dukes and earls, then knights, esquires and gentlemen, and below that the citizens. City merchants were able to make vast sums: Sir John Spencer, Sir William Craven and Sir Baptist Hicks each left legacies of over £100,000 (equivalent to a hundred times that amount in today's money). The professional classes such as doctors, clergymen and especially lawyers also remained secure and wealthy.

The City of London was still a medieval walled city, with its six gates locked at night; the Tower of London with its huge fortifications was secure in the south-east between the walls and the river, and London Bridge was the only way to cross the Thames other than paying the watermen who rowed across in ferries. Accommodation for the poor was cramped, filthy, and rat-infested, so the inhabitants readily succumbed to plague, with 25,000 dying from an epidemic in 1603 as well as about 5,000 deaths from other diseases.

Proclamations made by Elizabeth I and James I reveal the differences in their attitudes towards the poor. The prudent Queen Elizabeth issued a series of proclamations in the 1580s aiming to stop further development in the city. She was concerned about possible lawlessness, about the lack of sufficient food of decent quality at reasonable prices, and about the fact that too many people lived in poor, overcrowded housing so that diseases would spread. In 1596 Elizabeth ordered that the landed gentry who lived in London should return to their country estates to continue their traditional role of helping the poor after the bad harvests. A Poor Law providing a system of support for the most needy was passed in 1598.

In contrast, in 1603 the new king re-issued one of his proclamations from the safety of leafy Woodstock, away from the dangers to health of city life. In it he blamed the poor for the outbreak of plague, describing them as 'dissolute' and 'dangerous'. Unlike the late queen, he welcomed the landed gentry as courtiers (an issue reflected in *The Revenger's Tragedy*). The crucial bonds between landowners and their tenants and supporters were swept away, as nobles turned their attention to making more money by enclosing land for rent, by selling their titles, and by going to court to seek royal patronage.

In *The Revenger's Tragedy* Vindice speaks of *patrimonies washed a-pieces* (I.iii.51), and of land sold in order to buy fine clothing (II.i.214–215). When Vindice mentioned the name of his mistress Gloriana, the educated members of the audience would have immediately picked up the reference to the late queen: Gloriana was the name given by the poet Edmund Spenser to the character representing Elizabeth I in *The Faerie Queene* (see Interpretations page 200). The character of Castiza represents the bitter fate of the honest poor.

The new king wasted national reserves on luxuries such as jewels and the £100,000 spent on gifts for his favourites in 1607. At regular banquets hosted by the king and queen for courtiers, perhaps 24 dishes would be set out on a high table for pre-supper refreshments; then all dishes were replaced and renewed for supper itself. This extravagance is reflected in references to gluttony and feasting throughout *The Revenger's Tragedy*. James's court was also a place where drunkenness and adultery were common, as reflected in the behaviour of courtiers in the play.

The nation's judicial system was also corrupted, as is reflected in Middleton's play in the frequent linking of justice to gold (I.iv.61, II.iii.63, III.i.7). Although James declared that a tyrannical king was unfit for rule, he also made it plain that a king was above the law, and he proclaimed the 'divine right' of kings. He wrote in his 1598 essay *The True Lawe of Free Monarchies* that a king was the highest being on earth and had absolute power over his subjects. This contrasted with the views of certain nobles, who believed that a king should rule by the consent of his lords and with his subjects' agreement. James strengthened his personal power by promoting supporters and favourites such as Robert Carr (who was appointed Earl of Somerset) and George Villiers (Duke of Buckingham) to membership of the policy-making Privy Council. In thus undermining the English judicial and social systems, James brought great hardship to many of his subjects.

Middleton's theatre

Just four years before Middleton's birth, the first public theatre (called 'the Theatre') was opened in 1576. Several more soon followed: the Curtain, 1577; the Rose, 1587; the Swan, 1595; the Globe, 1599 (which replaced the Theatre), and the Fortune, 1600. There was also one innyard theatre, the Boar's Head, from 1599. Another innyard theatre, the Red Bull, was opened in 1605, and the Hope in 1613. In addition, there were two sophisticated indoor theatres for popular companies of boy actors, the Children of Paul's and the Children of the Chapel at Blackfriars, both refurbished and reopened in 1601.

The city judiciary regarded theatres as places of vice, and plays as potential threats to established authorities. To avoid constant harassment from disapproving officials, the new public theatres were built just outside the city walls. The Swan, Rose, Globe and Hope were built south of the River Thames at Bankside (see the map opposite); the Theatre and the Curtain were at Shoreditch to the north-east, while the Red Bull lay west of these in nearby Clerkenwell and the Boar's Head stood in Whitechapel. The indoor theatres faced no such official threats, since they stood in the grounds of former monasteries, on land belonging to the Church.

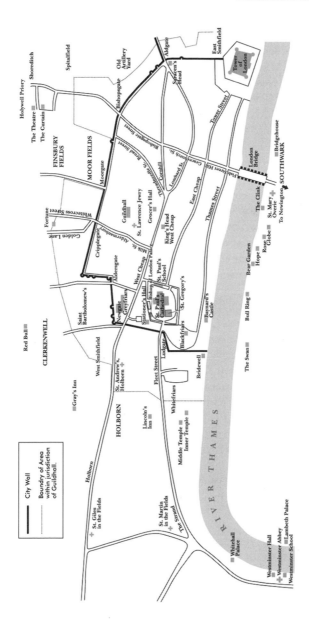

This map of Middleton's London shows his birthplace in Old Jewry and the theatres of the time

The two main acting companies, the Admiral's Men and the Chamberlain's Men, founded in the 1570s and 1590s respectively, each had a huge fan base. The Chamberlain's Men played at the Globe, presenting great plays such as Shakespeare's *Henry V* with star actor Richard Burbage, and the Admiral's Men offered equally attractive theatre such as Christopher Marlowe's *The Jew of Malta*, with their own star player, Edward Alleyn. Despite the disapproval of the authorities, two new companies were soon formed, the Earl of Derby's troupe at the Boar's Head and the Earl of Worcester's Men at the Rose. On the accession of James I, the Admiral's Men became known as Prince Henry's Men, and the Chamberlain's Men became the King's Men.

When Middleton chose a career as a playwright he would have known of the ups and downs of the theatre business. As well as stiff competition among themselves, and disapproval by the city authorities, the public theatre companies also faced recurrent closures during plague epidemics, for example in 1592–1594. The civic authorities also provided competition for the public theatres in the shape of the grand public pageants that attracted the same potential audience. As the companies needed to pay their running costs and recoup their spending on elaborate costumes and props, frequent performances with capacity audiences were essential to the theatres' finances. In a risky business, boldness was essential, as was shown when the landlord of the Theatre was causing problems over the lease. Seizing an opportunity during his absence for Christmas in 1598, the Burbage brothers with the Chamberlain's Men pulled down their theatre timber by timber, stored it over winter, and in spring 1599 rebuilt it as the Globe, on a new site next to their rivals, the Admiral's Men at the Rose.

Indoor theatres, despite their much smaller audience capacity, had an easier time, as they were not subject to the intervention of the city judiciary or the Privy Council. The Children of Paul's had been founded to showcase the vocal talents of the boy choristers, but their repertoire was gradually extended to include new plays. They became known for the quality of their productions, with a contemporary, often satirical programme, offering real competition to the public theatres. With the excuse of presenting 'public rehearsals', entry charges were imposed at both indoor theatres. These companies had great prestige, giving royal performances for both Elizabeth I and James I.

The English weather was also a challenge to the takings of the public theatres, as they were open to the elements. Entry charges ranged from the single penny charged to 'groundlings' who stood in the yard, to six pence for a seat in the most expensive box in the galleries. At the indoor theatres, customers of the Children of Paul's usually paid between two and six pence, and at Blackfriars people paid up to four times as much to sit at the edge of the stage and be seen.

The Jacobean playhouse had a 'thrust' stage extending into the audience, surrounded by two or three covered, tiered galleries (see the illustration overleaf and Interpretations pages 182–183). The stage varied in size from up to 1200 square feet in the public theatres to 500 at the indoor theatres. The cover over the stage was called the 'heavens', and 'hell' lay below the stage through a trap door. A carved, ornamental wooden backdrop supported a gallery as a raised area for acting, or as a discovery space where, for example, the presentation of Antonio's dead wife (I.iv) could be played. There were ladders, pulleys, ropes and a crane on the roof for special effects such as the *blazing star* (V.iii).

Actors became professionals, and entrepreneurs such as Philip Henslowe (who had built the Fortune and the Hope) created collaborative teams of writers from various backgrounds to supply the essential stream of new plays, which would belong to the company. To ensure that plays came in regularly and that standards did not slip, Henslowe would often pay in instalments. Although earlier playwrights such as Thomas Kyd, Marlowe and Shakespeare had made a good living, for Middleton and his contemporaries it was more difficult. To cut costs there were many revivals of established plays, and a playwright's old material might be re-used to avoid paying for new. So Middleton

The interior of Blackfriars Theatre in about 1600

varied his output as a writer. As well as writing plays for both of the leading companies, he wrote and supervised great court and civic masques, and for the Children of Paul's he wrote satiric city comedies such as *Michaelmas Term* (1604) and *A Trick to Catch the Old One* (1605), which drew packed audiences – even the monarch's wife, Queen Anne, attended.

Middleton's drama

Jacobean drama had varied literary sources, which are reflected in Middleton's plays. From traditional English drama there is evidence of the influence of mystery and morality plays and Tudor interludes. Middleton also shows the influence of Greek and Roman classical drama; both were fused in Elizabethan revenge tragedy. To this mix he added satire and other characteristics of contemporary plays.

Thirteenth-century mystery plays were traditionally played in cycles at fixed locations such as Chester and Wakefield, each individual episode portraying a biblical story. Shakespeare probably saw the Coventry cycle, last played in 1579. Later morality plays such as *Mankind* (1470) record humanity's progress towards salvation while encountering temptations and setbacks along the way, but do not echo biblical events as in the mystery plays. Their rise-and-fall pattern underpins early Renaissance tragedy, and they are wider in scope, reflecting broader social and political events. Both genres present vice and evil as comic; the Devil and his henchmen are mocked, as they are bound to be defeated, and they are shown to be absurd in their ambitious schemes. Evil is made laughable, because there is a belief in final redemption and salvation. In *The Revenger's Tragedy* Middleton similarly makes us laugh at wickedness, but without a clear scheme of moral certainties the evil appears more shocking (see *Horrid Laughter in Jacobean Tragedy* by Nicholas Brooke, Further Reading page 233).

The Revenger's Tragedy has many echoes of these earlier types of plays. There is an allegorical level of meaning in which certain characters are the representations of goodness or evil, while the Vice is the central figure. The plot charts the fall and punishment of the wicked characters, whose names usually indicate their function (see Interpretations page 151).

The Tudor interlude consisted of different kinds of dramatic representation: political, tragic, moral and biblical. Often played at court in intervals during another entertainment or a banquet, they usually had two or three episodes with two or more players. Again, the Vice is a central character; he might be a tempter or evil, but he will also be the agent of truth. In John Pickering's *A New Interlude of Vice Concerning the History of Horestes* (1567) the Vice figure admits that he represents both courage and revenge. Similarly, in *The Revenger's Tragedy* Vindice comments on moral weaknesses or evils both in himself and in other characters; he shapes the plot, has a special authority with the audience through direct address, and moves rapidly between emotional extremes.

There is evidence of the influence of the Greek classical drama of Sophocles in the creation of Vindice as a protagonist; he follows the classical tradition in that he is nobly born, suffers a fall and is ironically blind to his own weaknesses. Also, as in Greek drama, much of the play's dark humour arises from ironic reversals in the characters' fortunes (M.C. Bradbrook counted 22; see *Themes and Conventions of Elizabethan Tragedy*, Further Reading page 233).

Earlier English dramatic forms were fused in the type of revenge tragedy that first appeared with Kyd's play *The Spanish Tragedy* in about 1587. The influence of the Roman philosopher and playwright Seneca's 'theatre of blood' is evident in the violence that occurs during the play and at its denouement. Seneca also supplied the five-act structure, which covers the planning of revenge, anticipation of the act, initial confrontation of revenger and victim(s), delays and confusion, and ultimate completion. Crucially, Seneca's observation that power over oneself is more important than power over others was the wisdom that protagonists like Vindice struggled to achieve. Middleton develops the basic premise that the revenger, in seeking vengeance for acts of murder or treachery, is prepared to sacrifice himself but will achieve some restoration of moral, social and political order (see Interpretations page 166).

Writers use satire to present criticism of a person or institution, while disguising this to a greater or lesser extent through the use of comedy. Satire was practised by Roman poets such as Juvenal (early second century CE), whose work became popular in Middleton's time and influenced the fashion for this genre. Those in power felt threatened, as Jacobean satire suggested the ideal from which society deviated; Middleton clearly exposed the abuses of the court of James I (see page 9 and Interpretations pages 206–208). As Middleton's satirical writing is based on his own experiences in London, his characters are presented naturalistically; since action and situation on stage develop logically from what we discover about the characters, we accept the realism of the world he presents on stage.

Middleton also borrowed elements from various contemporary plays such as Marlowe's *Dr Faustus* (first performed between 1588 and 1592), which shows the temptation of Faustus and a parade of the Vices. Middleton's treatment of the revenger and the episodes with the skull are obviously influenced by Shakespeare's *Hamlet* (about 1601), while the idea of the schemer being trapped by his own intrigues may stem from the character of Mosca in Ben Jonson's *Volpone* (1606), and the character of the melancholic, brooding revenger owes much to John Marston's *The Malcontent* (1604). These influences are discussed further in Interpretations (page 158).

Finally, the play contains echoes of Middleton's contact with Calvinist beliefs (see Interpretations pages 178–179), according to which only God could choose which human beings would be saved, the so-called 'elect'; no one else could ever achieve salvation, no matter what they did. It is a nihilistic vision (one that suggests all human values are without foundation, and that we can never discover full truth or knowledge) which some readers feel pervades the play.

Middleton's influence may be seen in some twentieth- and twenty-first-century drama, such as Joe Orton's black farce and Samuel Beckett's stoical, perhaps noble, characters who struggle against the hopelessness of the human situation in an indifferent universe. The satire in *The Revenger's Tragedy* is extraordinarily forceful, economical and effective, perhaps because of the energy of Middleton's language and of his dramatic vision; it forces the audience to become involved in the questions it raises.

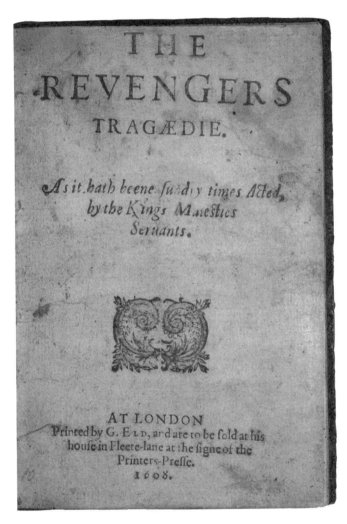

THE REVENGERS TRAGÆDIE.

As it hath beene sundry times Acted, by the Kings Maiesties Seruants.

AT LONDON
Printed by G. Eld, and are to be sold at his
house in Fleete-lane at the signe of the
Printers-Presse.
1608.

Title page of the 1608 edition of the play

The Persons of the Play

The Duke
Lussurioso, *the Duke's son by an earlier marriage, and heir*
Spurio, *his bastard son*
Ambitioso, *the Duchess's eldest son*
Supervacuo, *the Duchess's second son*
Junior Brother, *the youngest son of the Duchess*
Antonio and Piero, *noblemen of the Duke's court*
Vindice, *the revenger, sometimes disguised as* Piato
Hippolito, *his brother, also called* Carlo
Dondolo, *servant to Gratiana and Castiza*
Nencio and Sordido, *servants of Lussurioso*
Judges, Nobles, Gentlemen, Officers, a Prison-keeper, Guards, and Servants
The Duchess
Gratiana, *mother of Vindice, Hippolito, and Castiza*
Castiza, *sister of Vindice and Hippolito*

Act I Scene I

Enter Vindice, [holding a skull; then] the Duke,
Duchess, Lussurioso, Spurio, with a train, pass over
the stage with torchlight

VINDICE   Duke – royal lecher! Go, gray-haired adultery;
And thou his son, as impious steeped as he;
And thou his bastard true-begot in evil;
And thou his duchess that will do with devil;
Four ex'lent characters. – O, that marrowless age   5
Would stuff the hollow bones with damned desires,
And 'stead of heat kindle infernal fires
Within the spendthrift veins of a dry duke,
A parched and juiceless luxur. O God! one
That has scarce blood enough to live upon,   10
And he to riot it like a son and heir?
O, the thought of that
Turns my abusèd heartstrings into fret.
[*To the skull*] Thou sallow picture of my poisoned love,
My study's ornament, thou shell of death,   15
Once the bright face of my betrothèd lady,
When life and beauty naturally filled out
These ragged imperfections,
When two heaven-pointed diamonds were set
In those unsightly rings – then 'twas a face   20
So far beyond the artificial shine
Of any woman's bought complexion
That the uprightest man (if such there be,
That sin but seven times a day) broke custom
And made up eight with looking after her.   25
O she was able to ha' made a usurer's son
Melt all his patrimony in a kiss,
And what his father fifty years told

To have consumed, and yet his suit been cold.
But O, accursèd palace!   30
Thee when thou wert appareled in thy flesh
The old duke poisoned,
Because thy purer part would not consent
Unto his palsy-lust; for old men lustful
Do show like young men angry, eager, violent,   35
Outbid like their limited performances.
O 'ware an old man hot and vicious:
'Age, as in gold, in lust is covetous.'
Vengeance, thou murder's quit-rent, and whereby
Thou show'st thyself tenant to Tragedy,   40
O keep thy day, hour, minute, I beseech,
For those thou hast determined. Hum, who e'er knew
Murder unpaid? Faith, give Revenge her due,
Sh'as kept touch hitherto. Be merry, merry;
Advance thee, O thou terror to fat folks,   45
To have their costly three-piled flesh worn off
As bare as this – for banquets, ease, and laughter
Can make great men, as greatness goes by clay,
But wise men little are more great than they.
        Enter Hippolito
HIPPOLITO   Still sighing o'er death's vizard?
VINDICE   Brother, welcome;   50
    What comfort bring'st thou? how go things at court?
HIPPOLITO   In silk and silver, brother; never braver.
VINDICE   Puh,
    Thou play'st upon my meaning. Prithee say,
    Has that bald madam, Opportunity,   55
    Yet thought upon's? Speak, are we happy yet?
    Thy wrongs and mine are for one scabbard fit.
HIPPOLITO   It may prove happiness.
VINDICE   What is't may prove?
    Give me to taste.

HIPPOLITO   Give me your hearing then.
  You know my place at court.
VINDICE   Aye, the duke's chamber;   60
  But 'tis a marvel thou'rt not turned out yet!
HIPPOLITO   Faith, I have been shoved at, but 'twas still
    my hap
  To hold by th'duchess' skirt – you guess at that;
  Whom such a coat keeps up can ne'er fall flat.
  But to the purpose: 65
  Last evening, predecessor unto this,
  The duke's son warily inquired for me,
  Whose pleasure I attended. He began
  By policy to open and unhusk me
  About the time and common rumour;   70
  But I had so much wit to keep my thoughts
  Up in their built houses, yet afforded him
  An idle satisfaction without danger.
  But the whole aim and scope of his intent
  Ended in this: conjuring me in private   75
  To seek some strange-digested fellow forth,
  Of ill-contented nature, either disgraced
  In former times, or by new grooms displaced
  Since his stepmother's nuptials; such a blood,
  A man that were for evil only good –   80
  To give you the true word, some base-coined pander.
VINDICE   I reach you, for I know his heat is such,
  Were there as many concubines as ladies
  He would not be contained, he must fly out.
  I wonder how ill-featured, vile-proportioned   85
  That one should be, if she were made for woman,
  Whom at the insurrection of his lust
  He would refuse for once; heart, I think none,
  Next to a skull, though more unsound than one.
  Each face he meets he strongly dotes upon.   90

HIPPOLITO   Brother, y'ave truly spoke him.
  He knows not you, but I'll swear you know him.
VINDICE   And therefore I'll put on that knave for once,
  And be a right man then, a man o' th' time;
  For to be honest is not to be i' th' world.   95
  Brother, I'll be that strange-composèd fellow.
HIPPOLITO   And I'll prefer you, brother.
VINDICE   Go to, then;
  The small'st advantage fattens wrongèd men.
  It may point out Occasion; if I meet her,
  I'll hold her by the foretop fast enough,   100
  Or like the French mole heave up hair and all.
  I have a habit that will fit it quaintly.
  Here comes our mother.
HIPPOLITO   And sister.
VINDICE   We must coin.
  Women are apt, you know, to take false money,
  But I dare stake my soul for these two creatures –   105
  Only excuse excepted, that they'll swallow
  Because their sex is easy in belief.
     [*Enter Gratiana and Castiza*]
GRATIANA   What news from court, son Carlo?
HIPPOLITO   Faith, mother,
  'Tis whispered there the duchess' youngest son
  Has played a rape on Lord Antonio's wife.   110
GRATIANA   On that religious lady!
CASTIZA   Royal blood! Monster, he deserves to die,
  If Italy had no more hopes but he.
VINDICE   Sister, y'ave sentenced most direct and true;
  The law's a woman, and would she were you.   115
  Mother, I must take leave of you.
GRATIANA   Leave for what?
VINDICE   I intend speedy travel.
HIPPOLITO   That he does, madam.

GRATIANA   Speedy indeed!
VINDICE   For since my worthy father's funeral,
  My life's unnatural to me, e'en compelled,   120
  As if I lived now when I should be dead.
GRATIANA   Indeed, he was a worthy gentleman,
  Had his estate been fellow to his mind.
VINDICE   The duke did much deject him.
GRATIANA   Much!
VINDICE   Too much,
  And through disgrace oft smothered in his spirit   125
  When it would mount. Surely I think he died
  Of discontent, the nobleman's consumption.
GRATIANA   Most sure he did.
VINDICE   Did he? 'lack – you know all,
  You were his midnight secretary.
GRATIANA   No.
  He was too wise to trust me with his thoughts.   130
VINDICE   I'faith then, father, thou wast wise indeed:
  'Wives are but made to go to bed and feed.'
  Come mother, sister. You'll bring me onward, brother?
HIPPOLITO   I will.
VINDICE [*aside*]   I'll quickly turn into another.
      Exeunt

Act I Scene II

Enter the Duke, Lussurioso, the Duchess, Spurio,
Ambitioso and Supervacuo; Junior Brother brought out
with Officers [to stand trial] for the rape; two judges
DUKE   Duchess, it is your youngest son, we're sorry,
  His violent act has e'en drawn blood of honour
  And stained our honours;

Thrown ink upon the forehead of our state
Which envious spirits will dip their pens into   5
After our death, and blot us in our tombs.
For that which would seem treason in our lives
Is laughter when we're dead; who dares now whisper
That dares not then speak out, and e'en proclaim
With loud words and broad pens our closest shame.   10
[FIRST] JUDGE   Your grace hath spoke like to your silver
      years,
Full of confirmèd gravity; for what is it to have
A flattering false insculption on a tomb,
And in men's hearts reproach? The bowelled corpse
May be cered in, but, with free tongue I speak,   15
'The faults of great men through their cerecloths
      break.'
DUKE   They do; we're sorry for't. It is our fate
To live in fear and die to live in hate.
I leave him to your sentence; doom him, lords –
The fact is great – whilst I sit by and sigh.   20
DUCHESS [*kneels*]   My gracious lord, I pray be merciful.
Although his trespass far exceed his years,
Think him to be your own, as I am yours;
Call him not son-in-law. The law, I fear,
Will fall too soon upon his name and him;   25
Temper his fault with pity!
LUSSURIOSO   Good my lord,
Then 'twill not taste so bitter and unpleasant
Upon the judges' palate; for offenses
Gilt o'er with mercy show like fairest women,
Good only for their beauties, which washed off,   30
No sin is uglier.
AMBITIOSO   I beseech your grace,
Be soft and mild; let not relentless Law
Look with an iron forehead on our brother.

PURIO [*aside*]   He yields small comfort yet; hope he
    shall die.
  And if a bastard's wish might stand in force,   35
  Would all the court were turned into a corse.
DUCHESS   No pity yet? Must I rise fruitless then,
  A wonder in a woman? Are my knees
  Of such low metal that without respect –
FIRST JUDGE   Let the offender stand forth.   40
  'Tis the duke's pleasure that impartial doom
  Shall take fast hold of his unclean attempt.
  A rape! why, 'tis the very core of lust,
  Double adultery.
JUNIOR BROTHER   So, sir.
SECOND JUDGE   And which was worse,
  Committed on the Lord Antonio's wife,   45
  That general-honest lady. Confess, my lord,
  What moved you to't?
JUNIOR BROTHER   Why, flesh and blood, my lord.
  What should move men unto a woman else?
LUSSURIOSO   O do not jest thy doom; trust not an axe
  Or sword too far. The law is a wise serpent   50
  And quickly can beguile thee of thy life.
  Though marriage only has made thee my brother,
  I love thee so far, play not with thy death.
JUNIOR BROTHER   I thank you, troth; good admonitions,
    faith,
  If I'd the grace now to make use of them.   55
FIRST JUDGE   That lady's name has spread such a fair wing
  Over all Italy, that if our tongues
  Were sparing toward the fact, judgement itself
  Would be condemned and suffer in men's thoughts.
JUNIOR BROTHER   Well then, 'tis done, and it would
    please me well   60
  Were it to do again: sure she's a goddess,

For I'd no power to see her, and to live.
It falls out true in this, for I must die;
Her beauty was ordained to be my scaffold.
And yet, methinks I might be easier 'sessed –   6
My fault being sport, let me but die in jest.
FIRST JUDGE   This be the sentence –
DUCHESS   O keep't upon your tongue, let it not slip.
Death too soon steals out of a lawyer's lip.
Be not so cruel-wise!
FIRST JUDGE   Your grace must pardon us,   7
'Tis but the justice of the law.
DUCHESS   The law
Is grown more subtle than a woman should be.
SPURIO [*aside*]   Now, now he dies; rid 'em away!
DUCHESS [*aside*]   O what it is to have an old-cool duke,
To be as slack in tongue as in performance!   7
FIRST JUDGE   Confirmed, this be the doom irrevocable –
DUCHESS   O!
FIRST JUDGE   Tomorrow early –
DUCHESS   Pray be abed, my lord.
FIRST JUDGE   Your grace much wrongs yourself.
AMBITIOSO   No, 'tis that tongue,
Your too much right, does do us too much wrong.
FIRST JUDGE   Let that offender –
DUCHESS   Live, and be in health.   8
FIRST JUDGE   Be on a scaffold –
DUKE   Hold, hold, my lord!
SPURIO   Pox on 't,
What makes my dad speak now?
DUKE   We will defer the judgement till next sitting.
In the meantime let him be kept close prisoner.
Guard, bear him hence.
AMBITIOSO [*to Junior Brother*]   Brother, this makes for thee;   8
Fear not, we'll have a trick to set thee free.

JUNIOR BROTHER   [to Ambitioso and Supervacuo]
    Brother, I will expect it from you both,
    And in that hope I rest.
SUPERVACUO   Farewell, be merry.
        Exit [Junior Brother] with a Guard
SPURIO [aside]   Delayed, deferred – nay then, if judgement
        have
    Cold blood, flattery and bribes will kill it.   90
DUKE   About it then, my lords, with your best powers;
    More serious business calls upon our hours.
        Exeunt [all except] Duchess
DUCHESS   Was't ever known step-duchess was so mild
    And calm as I? Some now would plot his death
    With easy doctors, those loose-living men,   95
    And make his withered grace fall to his grave,
    And keep church better.
    Some second wife would do this, and dispatch
    Her double-loathèd lord at meat and sleep.
    Indeed 'tis true an old man's twice a child –   100
    Mine cannot speak. One of his single words
    Would quite have freed my youngest, dearest son
    From death or durance, and have made him walk
    With a bold foot upon the thorny law,
    Whose prickles should bow under him. But 'tis not,   105
    And therefore wedlock faith shall be forgot.
    I'll kill him in his forehead; hate, there feed;
    That wound is deepest, though it never bleed.
        [Enter Spurio]
    And here comes he whom my heart points unto,
    His bastard son, but my love's true-begot;   110
    Many a wealthy letter have I sent him,
    Swelled up with jewels, and the timorous man
    Is yet but coldly kind.
    That jewel's mine that quivers in his ear,

Mocking his master's chillness and vain fear. 115
H'as spied me now.
SPURIO   Madam, your grace so private?
My duty on your hand.
DUCHESS   Upon my hand, sir! Troth, I think you'd fear
To kiss my hand too if my lip stood there.
SPURIO   Witness I would not, madam.
      [*He kisses her*]
DUCHESS   'Tis a wonder, 120
For ceremony has made many fools.
It is as easy way unto a duchess
As to a hatted dame (if her love answer),
But that by timorous honours, pale respects,
Idle degrees of fear, men make their ways 125
Hard of themselves. What have you thought of me?
SPURIO   Madam, I ever think of you in duty,
Regard, and –
DUCHESS   Puh, upon my love, I mean.
SPURIO   I would 'twere love, but 'tis a fouler name
Than lust. You are my father's wife, 130
Your grace may guess now what I could call it.
DUCHESS   Why, th'art his son but falsely;
'Tis a hard question whether he begot thee.
SPURIO   I'faith, 'tis true too; I'm an uncertain man, of
more uncertain woman. Maybe his groom o' th' 135
stable begot me – you know I know not. He could
ride a horse well, a shrewd suspicion, marry! He was
wondrous tall, he had his length, i' faith, for peeping
over half-shut holiday windows. Men would desire
him 'light when he was afoot, he made a goodly show 140
under a penthouse, and when he rid, his hat would
check the signs, and clatter barbers' basins.
DUCHESS   Nay, set you a-horseback once, you'll ne'er
      'light off.

SPURIO   Indeed, I am a beggar.

DUCHESS   That's more the sign th'art great. But to our love: 145
　Let it stand firm both in thought and mind
　That the duke was thy father, as no doubt then
　He bid fair for't; thy injury is the more.
　For had he cut thee a right diamond,
　Thou hadst been next set in the dukedom's ring,   150
　When his worn self, like age's easy slave,
　Had dropped out of the collet into th' grave.
　What wrong can equal this? Canst thou be tame
　And think upon't?

SPURIO　　　　　　　No, mad and think upon't.

DUCHESS   Who would not be revenged of such a father,   155
　E'en in the worst way? I would thank that sin
　That could most injury him, and be in league with it.
　O what a grief 'tis, that a man should live
　But once i' th' world, and then to live a bastard,
　The curse o' the womb, the thief of nature,   160
　Begot against the seventh commandment,
　Half damned in the conception, by the justice
　Of that unbribèd, everlasting law.

SPURIO   O, I'd a hot-backed devil to my father.

DUCHESS   Would not this mad e'en patience, make
　　blood rough?   165
　Who but an eunuch would not sin, his bed
　By one false minute disinherited?

SPURIO [*aside*]   Aye, there's the vengeance that my birth
　　was wrapped in.
　I'll be revenged for all. Now hate begin;
　I'll call foul incest but a venial sin.   170

DUCHESS   Cold still! In vain then must a duchess woo?

SPURIO   Madam, I blush to say what I will do.

DUCHESS   Thence flew sweet comfort.
　　[*Kisses him*]

                            Earnest and farewell.

SPURIO   O, one incestuous kiss picks open hell.

DUCHESS   Faith, now, old duke, my vengeance shall
    reach high: 175
  I'll arm thy brow with woman's heraldry.
    Exit [*Duchess*]

SPURIO   Duke, thou didst do me wrong, and by thy act
  Adultery is my nature.
  Faith, if the truth were known, I was begot
  After some gluttonous dinner; some stirring dish   180
  Was my first father, when deep healths went round,
  And ladies' cheeks were painted red with wine,
  Their tongues, as short and nimble as their heels,
  Uttering words sweet and thick; and when they rose,
  Were merrily disposed to fall again.   185
  In such a whisp'ring and withdrawing hour,
  When base male-bawds kept sentinel at stair-head,
  Was I stol'n softly. O, damnation met
  The sin of feasts, drunken adultery.
  I feel it swell me. My revenge is just;   190
  I was begot in impudent wine and lust.
  Stepmother, I consent to thy desires;
  I love thy mischief well, but I hate thee,
  And those three cubs, thy sons, wishing confusion,
  Death, and disgrace may be their epitaphs.   195
  As for my brother, the duke's only son,
  Whose birth is more beholding to report
  Than mine, and yet perhaps as falsely sown
  (Women must not be trusted with their own),
  I'll loose my days upon him, hate all I.   200
  Duke, on thy brow I'll draw my bastardy.
  For indeed a bastard by nature should make cuckolds,
  Because he is the son of a cuckold-maker.
    Exit

Act I Scene III

Enter Vindice and Hippolito, Vindice in disguise [as Piato] to attend Lussurioso

VINDICE   What, brother? Am I far enough from myself?

HIPPOLITO   As if another man had been sent whole
Into the world, and none wist how he came.

VINDICE   It will confirm me bold, the child o' th' court.
Let blushes dwell i' th' country. Impudence,   5
Thou goddess of the palace, mistress of mistresses,
To whom the costly perfumed people pray,
Strike thou my forehead into dauntless marble,
Mine eyes to steady sapphires; turn my visage,
And if I must needs glow, let me blush inward,   10
That this immodest season may not spy
That scholar in my cheeks, fool-bashfulness,
That maid in the old time, whose flush of grace
Would never suffer her to get good clothes.
Our maids are wiser, and are less ashamed;   15
Save Grace the bawd, I seldom hear grace named!

HIPPOLITO   Nay, brother, you reach out o' th' verge
now. 'Sfoot, the duke's son; settle your looks.
[*Enter Lussurioso*]

VINDICE   Pray let me not be doubted.

HIPPOLITO   My lord –

LUSSURIOSO Hippolito? [*To Vindice*] Be absent, leave us.   20
[*Vindice withdraws to one side*]

HIPPOLITO   My lord, after long search, wary inquiries,
And politic siftings, I made choice of yon fellow,
Whom I guess rare for many deep employments.
This our age swims within him – and if Time
Had so much hair, I should take him for Time,   25
He is so near kin to this present minute.

LUSSURIOSO   'Tis enough.

We thank thee; yet words are but great men's blanks.
Gold, though it be dumb, does utter the best thanks.
[*Gives Hippolito money*]
HIPPOLITO   Your plenteous honour! An ex'lent fellow,
my lord.   30
LUSSURIOSO   So, give us leave.
[*Exit Hippolito*]
[*To Vindice*] Welcome, be not far off, we must be
better acquainted.
Push, be bold with us; thy hand.
VINDICE   With all my heart, i' faith.
[*Embraces Lussurioso*]
                                              How dost, sweet muskcat?
When shall we lie together?
LUSSURIOSO [*aside*]   Wondrous knave!   35
Gather him into boldness? 'Sfoot, the slave's
Already as familiar as an ague,
And shakes me at his pleasure. [*To Vindice*] Friend, I can
Forget myself in private, but elsewhere
I pray do you remember me.   40
VINDICE   O very well, sir – I conster myself saucy.
LUSSURIOSO   What hast been, of what profession?
VINDICE   A bone-setter.
LUSSURIOSO   A bone-setter?
VINDICE   A bawd, my lord; one that sets bones together.   45
LUSSURIOSO Notable bluntness!
Fit, fit for me, e'en trained up to my hand.
Thou hast been scrivener to much knavery, then?
VINDICE   Fool to abundance, sir; I have been witness to
the surrenders of a thousand virgins, and not so little.   50
I have seen patrimonies washed a-pieces, fruit fields
turned into bastards, and, in a world of acres, not so
much dust due to the heir 'twas left to, as would well
gravel a petition.

LUSSURIOSO [*aside*]   Fine villain! troth, I like him
     wondrously,   55
   He's e'en shaped for my purpose. [*To Vindice*] Then
     thou know'st
   I' th' world strange lust.
VINDICE   O Dutch lust! fulsome lust!
   Drunken procreation, which begets so many drunkards.
   Some father dreads not (gone to bed in wine)
   To slide from the mother, and cling the daughter-in-law;   60
   Some uncles are adulterous with their nieces,
   Brothers with brothers' wives. O hour of incest!
   Any kin now, next to the rim o' th' sister,
   Is man's meat in these days; and in the morning,
   When they are up and dressed and their mask on,   65
   Who can perceive this, save that eternal eye
   That sees through flesh and all? Well, if any thing
   Be damned, it will be twelve o'clock at night;
   That twelve will never 'scape:
   It is the Judas of the hours, wherein   70
   Honest salvation is betrayed to sin.
LUSSURIOSO   In troth, it is, too. But let this talk glide.
   It is our blood to err, though hell gaped loud;
   Ladies know Lucifer fell, yet still are proud.
   Now, sir, wert thou as secret as thou'rt subtle   75
   And deeply fathomed into all estates,
   I would embrace thee for a near employment,
   And thou shouldst swell in money, and be able
   To make lame beggars crouch to thee.
VINDICE   My lord,
   Secret? I ne'er had that disease o' th' mother,   80
   I praise my father. Why are men made close,
   But to keep thoughts in best? I grant you this,
   Tell but some woman a secret over night,
   Your doctor may find it in the urinal i' th' morning.

35

But, my lord –
LUSSURIOSO   So, thou'rt confirmed in me,   85
   And thus I enter thee.
      [*Gives money*]
VINDICE   This Indian devil
   Will quickly enter any man but a usurer:
   He prevents that by ent'ring the devil first.
LUSSURIOSO   Attend me: I am past my depth in lust,
   And I must swim or drown. All my desires   90
   Are levelled at a virgin not far from court,
   To whom I have conveyed by messenger
   Many waxed lines, full of my neatest spirit,
   And jewels that were able to ravish her
   Without the help of man; all which and more   95
   She, foolish chaste, sent back, the messengers
   Receiving frowns for answers.
VINDICE   Possible?
   'Tis a rare phoenix, whoe'er she be.
   If your desires be such, she so repugnant,
   In troth, my lord, I'd be revenged and marry her.   100
LUSSURIOSO   Push, the dowry of her blood and of her
      fortunes
   Are both too mean – good enough to be bad withal.
   I'm one of that number can defend
   Marriage is good, yet rather keep a friend.
   Give me my bed by stealth – there's true delight;   105
   What breeds a loathing in't, but night by night?
VINDICE   A very fine religion.
LUSSURIOSO   Therefore, thus,
   I'll trust thee in the business of my heart,
   Because I see thee well experienced
   In this luxurious day wherein we breathe.   110
   Go thou, and with a smooth enchanting tongue
   Bewitch her ears, and cozen her of all grace,

Enter upon the portion of her soul,
Her honour, which she calls her chastity,
And bring it into expense; for honesty   115
Is like a stock of money laid to sleep,
Which, ne'er so little broke, does never keep.
VINDICE   You have gi'en 't the tang, i'faith, my lord.
Make known the lady to me, and my brain
Shall swell with strange invention; I will move it   120
Till I expire with speaking, and drop down
Without a word to save me, but I'll work –
LUSSURIOSO   We thank thee, and will raise thee.
Receive her name: it is the only daughter to Madam
Gratiana, the late widow.   125
VINDICE [*aside*]   O, my sister, my sister!
LUSSURIOSO   Why dost walk aside?
VINDICE   My lord, I was thinking how I might begin,
As thus, 'O lady' – or twenty hundred devices;
Her very bodkin will put a man in.
LUSSURIOSO   Aye, or the wagging of her hair.   130
VINDICE   No, that shall put you in, my lord.
LUSSURIOSO   Shall't? Why, content. Dost know the
daughter then?
VINDICE   O, ex'lent well by sight.
LUSSURIOSO   That was her brother
That did prefer thee to us.
VINDICE   My lord, I think so;
I knew I had seen him somewhere –   135
LUSSURIOSO   And therefore prithee let thy heart to him
Be as a virgin, close.
VINDICE   O me, good lord.
LUSSURIOSO   We may laugh at that simple age within him.
VINDICE   Ha, ha, ha!
LUSSURIOSO   Himself being made the subtle instrument, 140
To wind up a good fellow –

VINDICE   That's I, my lord.
LUSSURIOSO   That's thou – to entice and work his sister.
VINDICE   A pure novice!
LUSSURIOSO   'Twas finely managed.
VINDICE   Gallantly carried; [*aside*] a pretty perfumed
    villain.
LUSSURIOSO   I've bethought me: 14⁵
    If she prove chaste still and immovable,
    Venture upon the mother, and with gifts
    As I will furnish thee, begin with her.
VINDICE   O fie, fie! that's the wrong end, my lord. 'Tis
    mere impossible that a mother by any gifts should   15⁰
    become a bawd to her own daughter!
LUSSURIOSO   Nay then, I see thou'rt but a puny in the
    subtle mystery of a woman.
    Why, 'tis held now no dainty dish: the name
    Is so in league with age, that nowadays   155
    It does eclipse three quarters of a mother.
VINDICE   Does't so, my lord?
    Let me alone then to eclipse the fourth.
LUSSURIOSO   Why, well said. Come, I'll furnish thee,
        but first
    Swear to be true in all.
VINDICE   True?
LUSSURIOSO   Nay, but swear.   16⁰
VINDICE   Swear? I hope your honour little doubts my
    faith.
LUSSURIOSO   Yet for my humour's sake, 'cause I love
    swearing.
VINDICE   'Cause you love swearing, 'slud, I will.
LUSSURIOSO   Why, enough.
    Ere long look to be made of better stuff.
VINDICE   That will do well indeed, my lord.
LUSSURIOSO   Attend me! 16⁵

[*Exit Lussurioso*]

VINDICE   O!
  Now let me burst, I've eaten noble poison.
  We are made strange fellows, brother: innocent villains.
  Wilt not be angry when thou hear'st on't, think'st thou?
  I'faith, thou shalt. Swear me to foul my sister!   170
      [*Unsheathes his sword*]
  Sword, I durst make a promise of him to thee:
  Thou shalt disheir him; it shall be thine honour.
  And yet, now angry froth is down in me,
  It would not prove the meanest policy
  In this disguise to try the faith of both.   175
  Another might have had the selfsame office –
  Some slave, that would have wrought effectually,
  Aye, and perhaps o'erwrought 'em. Therefore I,
  Being thought travelled, will apply myself
  Unto the selfsame form, forget my nature,   180
  As if no part about me were kin to 'em;
  So touch 'em – though I durst, almost for good,
  Venture my lands in heaven upon their blood.
      Exit

Act I Scene IV

Enter the discontented Lord Antonio, whose wife the
Duchess's youngest son ravished; he discovering the
body of her dead to certain lords [including Piero,]
and Hippolito

ANTONIO   Draw nearer, lords, and be sad witnesses
  Of a fair, comely building newly fall'n,
  Being falsely undermined. Violent rape
  Has played a glorious act. Behold, my lords,

A sight that strikes man out of me.
PIERO   That virtuous lady!
ANTONIO   Precedent for wives!
HIPPOLITO   The blush of many women, whose chaste
    presence
  Would e'en call shame up to their cheeks, and make
  Pale wanton sinners have good colours.
ANTONIO   Dead!
  Her honour first drunk poison, and her life,   10
  Being fellows in one house, did pledge her honour.
PIERO   O grief of many!
ANTONIO   I marked not this before –
  A prayer-book the pillow to her cheek;
  This was her rich confection, and another
  Placed in her right hand, with a leaf tucked up,   15
  Pointing to these words:
  '*Melius virtute mori, quam per dedecus vivere.*'
  True and effectual it is indeed.
HIPPOLITO   My lord, since you invite us to your sorrows,
  Let's truly taste 'em, that with equal comfort,   20
  As to ourselves, we may relieve your wrongs;
  We have grief too, that yet walks without tongue –
  Curae leves loquuntur, majores stupent.
ANTONIO   You deal with truth, my lord.
  Lend me but your attentions, and I'll cut   25
  Long grief into short words. Last revelling night,
  When torchlight made an artificial noon
  About the court, some courtiers in the masque,
  Putting on better faces than their own
  (Being full of fraud and flattery), amongst whom   30
  The duchess' youngest son (that moth to honour)
  Filled up a room; and with long lust to eat
  Into my wearing, amongst all the ladies
  Singled out that dear form, who ever lived

As cold in lust as she is now in death   35
(Which that step-duchess' monster knew too well);
And therefore in the height of all the revels,
When music was heard loudest, courtiers busiest,
And ladies great with laughter – O vicious minute,
Unfit but for relation to be spoke of! –   40
Then, with a face more impudent than his vizard,
He harried her amidst a throng of panders
That live upon damnation of both kinds,
And fed the ravenous vulture of his lust.
O death to think on't! She, her honour forced,   45
Deemed it a nobler dowry for her name
To die with poison than to live with shame.

HIPPOLITO   A wondrous lady, of rare fire compact;
 Sh'as made her name an empress by that act.

PIERO   My lord, what judgement follows the offender?   50

ANTONIO   Faith, none, my lord; it cools and is deferred.

PIERO   Delay the doom for rape?

ANTONIO   O, you must note who 'tis should die,
 The duchess' son. She'll look to be a saver:
 'Judgement in this age is near kin to favour.'   55

HIPPOLITO   Nay then, step forth, thou bribeless officer.
  [*He draws his sword*]
 I bind you all in steel to bind you surely;
 Here let your oaths meet, to be kept and paid,
 Which else will stick like rust, and shame the blade.
 Strengthen my vow, that if at the next sitting   60
 Judgement speak all in gold, and spare the blood
 Of such a serpent, e'en before their seats
 To let his soul out, which long since was found
 Guilty in heaven.

ALL   We swear it and will act it.

ANTONIO   Kind gentlemen, I thank you in mine ire.   65

HIPPOLITO   'Twere pity

41

The ruins of so fair a monument
Should not be dipped in the defacer's blood.
PIERO   Her funeral shall be wealthy, for her name
Merits a tomb of pearl. My Lord Antonio,   7c
For this time wipe your lady from your eyes;
No doubt our grief and yours may one day court it,
When we are more familiar with revenge.
ANTONIO   That is my comfort, gentlemen, and I joy
In this one happiness above the rest,   7⁵
Which will be called a miracle at last:
That being an old man, I'd a wife so chaste.
    Exeunt

Act II Scene I

Enter Castiza

CASTIZA   How hardly shall that maiden be beset,
Whose only fortunes are her constant thoughts,
That has no other child's-part but her honour
That keeps her low and empty in estate.
Maids and their honours are like poor beginners;   5
Were not sin rich, there would be fewer sinners.
Why had not virtue a revenue? Well,
I know the cause, 'twould have impoverished hell.
    [*Enter Dondolo*]
How now, Dondolo?

DONDOLO   Madonna, there is one, as they say, a thing   10
of flesh and blood, a man I take him by his beard,
that would very desirously mouth to mouth with
you.

CASTIZA   What's that?

DONDOLO   Show his teeth in your company.   15

CASTIZA   I understand thee not.

DONDOLO   Why, speak with you, madonna!

CASTIZA   Why, say so, madman, and cut off a great deal
of dirty way; had it not been better spoke in ordinary
words, that one would speak with me?   20

DONDOLO   Ha, ha, that's as ordinary as two shillings. I
would strive a little to show myself in my place; a
gentleman-usher scorns to use the phrase and fancy of
a servingman.

CASTIZA   Yours be your own, sir; go direct him hither.   25
    [*Exit Dondolo*]
I hope some happy tidings from my brother
That lately travelled, whom my soul affects.
Here he comes.

Enter Vindice, disguised

VINDICE   Lady, the best of wishes to your sex –
Fair skins and new gowns.
    [*Gives her a letter*]
CASTIZA   O, they shall thank you, sir.   3
    Whence this?
VINDICE   O, from a dear and worthy friend,
    Mighty!
CASTIZA   From whom?
VINDICE   The duke's son!
CASTIZA   Receive that!
    Gives a box o' th' ear to Vindice
    I swore I'd put anger in my hand,
    And pass the virgin limits of my self,
    To him that next appeared in that base office,   3
    To be his sin's attorney. Bear to him
    That figure of my hate upon thy cheek
    Whilst 'tis yet hot, and I'll reward thee for't;
    Tell him my honour shall have a rich name,
    When several harlots shall share his with shame.   4
    Farewell! Commend me to him in my hate.
    Exit [*Castiza*]
VINDICE   It is the sweetest box that e'er my nose came
        nigh,
    The finest drawn-work cuff that e'er was worn;
    I'll love this blow forever, and this cheek
    Shall still henceforward take the wall of this.   4
    O, I'm above my tongue! Most constant sister,
    In this thou hast right honourable shown;
    Many are called by their honour that have none.
    Thou art approved forever in my thoughts.
    It is not in the power of words to taint thee;   5
    And yet for the salvation of my oath,
    As my resolve in that point, I will lay

Hard siege unto my mother, though I know
A siren's tongue could not bewitch her so.
   [*Enter Gratiana*]
Mass, fitly here she comes; thanks, my disguise.   55
– Madam, good afternoon.
GRATIANA   Y'are welcome, sir!
VINDICE   The next of Italy commends him to you,
  Our mighty expectation, the duke's son.
GRATIANA   I think myself much honoured that he pleases
  To rank me in his thoughts.
VINDICE   So may you, lady: 60
  One that is like to be our sudden duke;
  The crown gapes for him every tide, and then
  Commander o'er us all. Do but think on him;
  How blest were they now that could pleasure him,
  E'en with anything almost.
GRATIANA   Aye, save their honour.   65
VINDICE   Tut, one would let a little of that go, too,
  And ne'er be seen in't: ne'er be seen in't, mark you.
  I'd wink and let it go –
GRATIANA   Marry, but I would not.
VINDICE   Marry, but I would, I hope; I know you
    would too,
  If you'd that blood now which you gave your daughter. 70
  To her indeed 'tis, this wheel comes about;
  That man that must be all this, perhaps ere morning
  (For his white father does but mould away),
  Has long desired your daughter.
GRATIANA   Desired?
VINDICE   Nay, but hear me: 75
  He desires now that will command hereafter.
  Therefore be wise – I speak as more a friend
  To you than him. Madam, I know y'are poor,
  And, 'lack the day, there are too many poor ladies already.

Why should you vex the number? 'tis despised!   8⟨
Live wealthy, rightly understand the world,
And chide away that foolish country girl
Keeps company with your daughter, Chastity.
GRATIANA   O fie, fie, the riches of the world cannot hire
A mother to such a most unnatural task.   8⟨
VINDICE   No, but a thousand angels can;
Men have no power, angels must work you to 't.
The world descends into such base-born evils
That forty angels can make fourscore devils.
There will be fools still, I perceive, still fools.   9⟨
Would I be poor, dejected, scorned of greatness,
Swept from the palace, and see other daughters
Spring with the dew o' th' court, having mine own
So much desired and loved – by the duke's son?
No, I would raise my state upon her breast,   9⟨
And call her eyes my tenants; I would count
My yearly maintenance upon her cheeks,
Take coach upon her lip; and all her parts
Should keep men after men, and I would ride
In pleasure upon pleasure.   10⟨
You took great pains for her, once when it was;
Let her requite it now, though it be but some.
You brought her forth; she may well bring you home.
GRATIANA   O heavens! this overcomes me.
VINDICE [*aside*]   Not, I hope, already!   10
GRATIANA [*aside*]   It is too strong for me, men know
        that know us,
We are so weak their words can overthrow us.
He touched me nearly, made my virtues bate,
When his tongue struck upon my poor estate.
VINDICE [*aside*]   I e'en quake to proceed, my spirit
        turns edge!   11⟨
I fear me she's unmothered, yet I'll venture:

'That woman is all male, whom none can enter.' –
What think you now, lady? Speak, are you wiser?
What said advancement to you? Thus it said:
The daughter's fall lifts up the mother's head.   115
Did it not, madam? But I'll swear it does
In many places; tut, this age fears no man.
' 'Tis no shame to be bad, because 'tis common.'
GRATIANA   Aye, that's the comfort on't.
VINDICE   The comfort on't!
I keep the best for last; can these persuade you   120
To forget heaven, and –
    [Gives her money]
GRATIANA   Aye, these are they –
VINDICE [aside]   O!
GRATIANA   – that enchant our sex; these are the means
    That govern our affections. That woman
    Will not be troubled with the mother long,
    That sees the comfortable shine of you: 125
    I blush to think what for your sakes I'll do.
VINDICE [aside]   O suff'ring heaven, with thy invisible
        finger
    E'en at this instant turn the precious side
    Of both mine eyeballs inward, not to see myself.
GRATIANA   Look you, sir.
VINDICE   Holla.
GRATIANA   Let this thank your pains.   130
    [Tips him]
VINDICE   O, y'are a kind madam.
GRATIANA   I'll see how I can move.
VINDICE   Your words will sting.
GRATIANA   If she be still chaste, I'll ne'er call her mine.
VINDICE [aside]   Spoke truer than you meant it.
GRATIANA   Daughter Castiza!
    [Enter Castiza]

47

CASTIZA   Madam?   13·

VINDICE   O, she's yonder; meet her. –
  [*Aside*] Troops of celestial soldiers guard her heart;
  Yon dam has devils enough to take her part.

CASTIZA   Madam, what makes yon evil-officed man
  In presence of you?

GRATIANA   Why?

CASTIZA   He lately brought   14·
  Immodest writing sent from the duke's son
  To tempt me to dishonourable act.

GRATIANA   Dishonourable act? Good honourable fool,
  That wouldst be honest 'cause thou wouldst be so,
  Producing no one reason but thy will.   14·
  And 't'as good report, prettily commended,
  But pray, by whom? – mean people, ignorant people;
  The better sort, I'm sure, cannot abide it.
  And by what rule should we square out our lives,
  But by our betters' actions? O, if thou knew'st   15·
  What 'twere to lose it, thou would never keep it.
  But there's a cold curse laid upon all maids,
  Whilst others clip the sun they clasp the shades.
  Virginity is paradise, locked up.
  You cannot come by your selves without fee,   15·
  And 'twas decreed that man should keep the key.
  Deny advancement, treasure, the duke's son?

CASTIZA   I cry you mercy, lady, I mistook you;
  Pray, did you see my mother? Which way went you?
  Pray God I have not lost her.

VINDICE   [*aside*]   Prettily put by.   16·

GRATIANA   Are you as proud to me as coy to him?
  Do you not know me now?

CASTIZA   Why, are you she?
  The world's so changed, one shape into another,
  It is a wise child now that knows her mother!

48

VINDICE [*aside*]   Most right, i' faith.

GRATIANA   I owe your cheek my hand   165
    For that presumption now, but I'll forget it.
    Come, you shall leave those childish 'haviours,
    And understand your time. Fortunes flow to you;
    What, will you be a girl?
    If all feared drowning that spy waves ashore,   170
    Gold would grow rich, and all the merchants poor.

CASTIZA   It is a pretty saying of a wicked one;
    But methinks now
    It does not show so well out of your mouth;
    Better in his.

VINDICE [*aside*]   Faith, bad enough in both,   175
    Were I in earnest, as I'll seem no less.
    [*To Castiza*] I wonder, lady, your own mother's words
    Cannot be taken, nor stand in full force.
    'Tis honesty you urge; what's honesty?
    'Tis but heaven's beggar;   180
    And what woman is so foolish to keep honesty,
    And be not able to keep herself? No,
    Times are grown wiser and will keep less charge.
    A maid that has small portion now intends
    To break up house and live upon her friends.   185
    How blest are you! You have happiness alone.
    Others must fall to thousands, you to one,
    Sufficient in himself to make your forehead
    Dazzle the world with jewels, and petitionary people
    Start at your presence.

GRATIANA   O, if I were young,   190
    I should be ravished.

CASTIZA   Aye, to lose your honour.

VINDICE   'Slid, how can you lose your honour
    To deal with my lord's grace?
    He'll add more honour to it by his title –

Your mother will tell you how.
GRATIANA   That I will.   19$
VINDICE   O, think upon the pleasure of the palace:
  Securèd ease and state; the stirring meats
  Ready to move out of the dishes,
  That e'en now quicken when they're eaten;
  Banquets abroad by torchlight, musics, sports;   20c
  Bareheaded vassals, that had ne'er the fortune
  To keep on their own hats, but let horns wear 'em;
  Nine coaches waiting – hurry, hurry, hurry!
CASTIZA   Aye, to the devil.
VINDICE [*aside*]   Aye, to the devil. – [*Aloud*] To th' duke,
    by my faith.   20$
GRATIANA   Aye, to the duke! Daughter, you'd scorn to
  think o' th' devil, an you were there once.
VINDICE [*aside*]   True, for most there are as proud as he
  for his heart, i'faith. –
  [*Aloud*] Who'd sit at home in a neglected room,   21c
  Dealing her short-lived beauty to the pictures
  That are as useless as old men, when those
  Poorer in face and fortune than herself
  Walk with a hundred acres on their backs,
  Fair meadows cut into green foreparts? – O,   21$
  It was the greatest blessing ever happened to women,
  When farmers' sons agreed, and met again
  To wash their hands, and come up gentlemen;
  The commonwealth has flourished ever since.
  Lands that were mete by the rod, that labour's spared; 22c
  Tailors ride down, and measure 'em by the yard.
  Fair trees, those comely foretops of the field,
  Are cut to maintain head-tires – much untold;
  All thrives but chastity; she lies a-cold.
  Nay, shall I come nearer to you? Mark but this: 22$

Why are there so few honest women, but because 'tis
the poorer profession? That's accounted best, that's
best followed – least in trade, least in fashion – and
that's not honesty, believe it.
And do but note the low and dejected price of it: 230
'Lose but a pearl, we search and cannot brook it;
But that once gone, who is so mad to look it?'

GRATIANA   Troth, he says true.

CASTIZA   False! I defy you both.
I have endured you with an ear of fire;
Your tongues have struck hot irons on my face.   235
Mother, come from that poisonous woman there!

GRATIANA   Where?

CASTIZA   Do you not see her? She's too inward then.
[*To Vindice*] Slave, perish in thy office! You heavens,
    please
Henceforth to make the mother a disease,
Which first begins with me; yet I've outgone you.   240
        Exit [*Castiza*]

VINDICE [*aside*]   O angels, clap your wings upon the skies,
And give this virgin crystal plaudities!

GRATIANA   Peevish, coy, foolish! – but return this answer:
My lord shall be most welcome, when his pleasure
Conducts him this way. I will sway mine own.   245
Women with women can work best alone.

VINDICE   Indeed, I'll tell him so.
        Exit [*Gratiana*]
O, more uncivil, more unnatural
Than those base-titled creatures that look downward!
Why does not heaven turn black, or with a frown   250
Undo the world? Why does not earth start up
And strike the sins that tread upon't? O,
Were't not for gold and women, there would be no
    damnation;

Hell would look like a lord's great kitchen without
    fire in't.
But 'twas decreed before the world began,   255
That they should be the hooks to catch at man.
    Exit

Act II Scene II

    Enter Lussurioso with Hippolito
LUSSURIOSO   I much applaud thy judgement.
  Thou art well read in a fellow,
  And 'tis the deepest art to study man.
  I know this, which I never learnt in schools:
  The world's divided into knaves and fools.   5
HIPPOLITO [*aside*]   Knave in your face, my lord – behind
  your back.
LUSSURIOSO   And I much thank thee that thou hast
  preferred
  A fellow of discourse, well mingled,
  And whose brain time hath seasoned.
HIPPOLITO   True, my lord.
  [*Aside*] We shall find season once, I hope. O villain,   10
  To make such an unnatural slave of me! but –
    [*Enter Vindice, disguised*]
LUSSURIOSO   Mass, here he comes.
HIPPOLITO [*aside*]   And now shall I have free leave to
  depart.
LUSSURIOSO   Your absence, leave us.
HIPPOLITO   [*aside*]   Are not my thoughts true?
  I must remove, but brother, you may stay.   15
  Heart, we are both made bawds a new-found way!
    Exit [*Hippolito*]

LUSSURIOSO   Now we're an even number. A third man's
　　dangerous,
　Especially her brother; say, be free,
　Have I a pleasure toward?
VINDICE 　　　　　　　　O my lord!
LUSSURIOSO   Ravish me in thine answer; art thou rare?　　20
　Hast thou beguiled her of salvation,
　And rubbed hell o'er with honey? Is she a woman?
VINDICE   In all but in desire.
LUSSURIOSO 　　　　　　　Then she's in nothing –
　I bate in courage now.
VINDICE 　　　　　　　The words I brought
　Might well have made indifferent-honest naught.　　25
　A right good woman in these days is changed
　Into white money with less labour far.
　Many a maid has turned to Mahomet
　With easier working; I durst undertake,
　Upon the pawn and forfeit of my life,　　　　　　30
　With half those words to flat a Puritan's wife.
　But she is close and good – yet 'tis a doubt
　By this time. O, the mother, the mother!
LUSSURIOSO   I never thought their sex had been a
　　wonder
　Until this minute. What fruit from the mother?　　35
VINDICE [*aside*]   Now must I blister my soul, be
　　forsworn,
　Or shame the woman that received me first.
　I will be true, thou liv'st not to proclaim:
　Spoke to a dying man, shame has no shame. –
　My lord.
LUSSURIOSO   Who's that?
VINDICE 　　　　　　　Here's none but I, my lord.　　40
LUSSURIOSO   What would thy haste utter?
VINDICE 　　　　　　　　　　　Comfort.

LUSSURIOSO   Welcome.
VINDICE   The maid being dull, having no mind to travel
  Into unknown lands, what did me I straight,
  But set spurs to the mother? Golden spurs
  Will put her to a false gallop in a trice.   45
LUSSURIOSO   Is't possible that in this
  The mother should be damned before the daughter?
VINDICE   O, that's good manners, my lord; the mother
  for her age must go foremost, you know.
LUSSURIOSO   Thou'st spoke that true! but where comes
    in this comfort?   50
VINDICE   In a fine place, my lord. The unnatural mother
  Did with her tongue so hard beset her honour,
  That the poor fool was struck to silent wonder.
  Yet still the maid, like an unlighted taper,
  Was cold and chaste, save that her mother's breath   55
  Did blow fire on her cheeks. The girl departed,
  But the good ancient madam, half mad, threw me
  These promising words, which I took deeply note of:
  'My lord shall be most welcome – '
LUSSURIOSO   Faith, I thank her.
VINDICE   'When his pleasure conducts him this way – '   60
LUSSURIOSO   That shall be soon, i' faith.
VINDICE   'I will sway mine own – '
LUSSURIOSO   She does the wiser; I commend her for't.
VINDICE   'Women with women can work best alone.'
LUSSURIOSO By this light, and so they can. Give 'em
  their due, men are not comparable to 'em.   65
VINDICE   No, that's true; for you shall have one woman
  knit more in an hour than any man can ravel again in
  seven-and-twenty year.
LUSSURIOSO   Now my desires are happy; I'll make 'em
  freemen now.   70
  Thou art a precious fellow; faith, I love thee.

Be wise and make it thy revenue: beg, leg!
What office couldst thou be ambitious for?
VINDICE   Office, my lord? Marry, if I might have my
   wish, I would have one that was never begged yet.   75
LUSSURIOSO   Nay, then thou canst have none.
VINDICE   Yes, my lord, I could pick out another office
   yet; nay, and keep a horse and drab upon 't.
LUSSURIOSO   Prithee, good bluntness, tell me.
VINDICE   Why, I would desire but this, my lord: to have   80
   all the fees behind the arras, and all the farthingales that
   fall plump about twelve o'clock at night upon the
   rushes.
LUSSURIOSO   Thou'rt a mad, apprehensive knave. Dost
   think to make any great purchase of that?   85
VINDICE   O, 'tis an unknown thing, my lord; I wonder
   't 'as been missed so long!
LUSSURIOSO   Well, this night I'll visit her, and 'tis till
      then
A year in my desires. Farewell. Attend;
Trust me with thy preferment.
VINDICE   My loved lord.   90
      Exit [Lussurioso. Vindice puts his hand to his sword]
O, shall I kill him o' th' wrong side now? No!
Sword, thou wast never a backbiter yet.
I'll pierce him to his face; he shall die looking upon me.
Thy veins are swelled with lust, this shall unfill 'em:
Great men were gods, if beggars could not kill 'em.   95
Forgive me, heaven, to call my mother wicked.
O, lessen not my days upon the earth;
I cannot honour her. By this, I fear me,
Her tongue has turned my sister into use.
I was a villain not to be forsworn   100
To this our lecherous hope, the duke's son;
For lawyers, merchants, some divines, and all

Count beneficial perjury a sin small.
It shall go hard yet, but I'll guard her honour,
And keep the ports sure.   10⁵

Enter Hippolito

HIPPOLITO Brother, how goes the world? I would know news
Of you, but I have news to tell you.

VINDICE What, in the name of knavery?

HIPPOLITO   Knavery, faith:
This vicious old duke's worthily abused.
The pen of his bastard writes him cuckold!   110

VINDICE His bastard?

HIPPOLITO   Pray believe it; he and the duchess
By night meet in their linen; they have been seen
By stair-foot panders.

VINDICE   O sin foul and deep!
Great faults are winked at when the duke's asleep.

[*Enter Spurio with two Servants*]

See, see, here comes the Spurio.

HIPPOLITO   Monstrous luxur!   115

VINDICE Unbraced, two of his valiant bawds with him.

[*Spurio and his servants talk apart*]

O, there's a wicked whisper; hell is in his ear.
Stay, let's observe his passage.

[*Vindice and Hippolito withdraw to one side*]

SPURIO O, but are you sure on't?

SERVANT My lord, most sure on't, for 'twas spoke by one   120
That is most inward with the duke's son's lust:
That he intends within this hour to steal
Unto Hippolito's sister, whose chaste life
The mother has corrupted for his use.

SPURIO Sweet word, sweeter occasion! Faith then, brother,   125
I'll disinherit you in as short time

As I was when I was begot in haste;
I'll damn you at your pleasure. Precious deed!
After your lust, O, 'twill be fine to bleed.
Come, let our passing out be soft and wary.   130
    Exeunt [Spurio and Servants]
VINDICE   Mark! there, there, that step, now to the
    duchess.
This, their second meeting, writes the duke cuckold
With new additions, his horns newly revived.
Night, thou that look'st like funeral herald's fees
Torn down betimes i' th' morning, thou hang'st fitly   135
To grace those sins that have no grace at all.
Now 'tis full sea abed over the world,
There's juggling of all sides; some that were maids
E'en at sunset are now perhaps i' th' toll-book.
This woman in immodest thin apparel   140
Lets in her friend by water; here a dame,
Cunning, nails leather hinges to a door
To avoid proclamation. Now cuckolds are
A-coining, apace, apace, apace, apace!
And careful sisters spin that thread i' th' night   145
That does maintain them and their bawds i' th' day.
HIPPOLITO   You flow well, brother.
VINDICE   Puh, I'm shallow yet,
Too sparing and too modest. Shall I tell thee?
If every trick were told that's dealt by night,
There are few here that would not blush outright.   150
HIPPOLITO   I am of that belief, too.
VINDICE   Who's this comes?
    [Enter Lussurioso]
The duke's son up so late? Brother, fall back,
And you shall learn some mischief.
    [Hippolito withdraws to one side]
                                – My good lord.

LUSSURIOSO   Piato! why, the man I wished for! Come,
  I do embrace this season for the fittest   155
  To taste of that young lady.
VINDICE [*aside*]   Heart and hell!
HIPPOLITO [*aside*]   Damned villain.
VINDICE [*aside*]   I ha' no way now to cross it but to kill him.
LUSSURIOSO   Come, only thou and I.
VINDICE   My lord, my lord!
LUSSURIOSO   Why dost thou start us?   160
VINDICE   I'd almost forgot – the bastard!
LUSSURIOSO   What of him?
VINDICE   This night, this hour – this minute, now –
LUSSURIOSO   What, what?
VINDICE   Shadows the duchess –
LUSSURIOSO   Horrible word!
VINDICE   And, like strong poison, eats
  Into the duke your father's forehead.
LUSSURIOSO   O!   165
VINDICE   He makes horn royal.
LUSSURIOSO   Most ignoble slave!
VINDICE   This is the fruit of two beds.
LUSSURIOSO   I am mad.
VINDICE   That passage he trod warily –
LUSSURIOSO   He did!
VINDICE   And hushed his villains every step he took.
LUSSURIOSO   His villains? I'll confound them.   170
VINDICE   Take 'em finely, finely now.
LUSSURIOSO   The duchess' chamber-door shall not
      control me.
        Exeunt [Lussurioso and Vindice]
HIPPOLITO   Good, happy, swift! There's gunpowder i' th'
      court,
  Wildfire at midnight. In this heedless fury

He may show violence to cross himself.   175
I'll follow the event.
> *Exit*

Act II Scene III

> *Enter again [Lussurioso and Vindice; the Duke and
> the Duchess in bed]*

LUSSURIOSO   Where is that villain?

VINDICE   Softly, my lord, and you may take 'em twisted.

LUSSURIOSO   I care not how!

VINDICE   O, 'twill be glorious
To kill 'em doubled, when they're heaped. Be soft, my
  lord.

LUSSURIOSO   Away, my spleen is not so lazy; thus, and
  thus,   5
I'll shake their eyelids ope, and with my sword
Shut 'em again forever.
> *[Lussurioso draws his sword]*
                              – Villain! strumpet!

DUKE   You upper guard, defend us!

DUCHESS   Treason, treason!

DUKE   O, take me not in sleep; I have great sins.
I must have days –   10
Nay, months, dear son, with penitential heaves,
To lift 'em out, and not to die unclear.
O, thou wilt kill me both in heaven and here.

LUSSURIOSO   I am amazed to death.

DUKE   Nay, villain, traitor,
Worse than the foulest epithet, now I'll gripe thee   15
E'en with the nerves of wrath, and throw thy head
Amongst the lawyers. Guard!

[Guards enter and seize Lussurioso.] Enter Nobles,
[Hippolito,] Ambitioso, and Supervacuo

FIRST NOBLE   How comes the quiet of your grace
disturbed?

DUKE   This boy, that should be myself after me,
Would be myself before me, and in heat   20
Of that ambition bloodily rushed in,
Intending to depose me in my bed.

SECOND NOBLE   Duty and natural loyalty forfend!

DUCHESS   He called his father villain, and me strumpet,
A word that I abhor to file my lips with.   25

AMBITIOSO   That was not so well done, brother.

LUSSURIOSO   I am abused –
I know there's no excuse can do me good.

VINDICE *[aside to Hippolito]*   'Tis now good policy to be
from sight.
His vicious purpose to our sister's honour
Is crossed, beyond our thought.

HIPPOLITO *[aside to Vindice]*   You little dreamt   30
His father slept here.

VINDICE *[aside to Hippolito]*   O, 'twas far beyond me.
But since it fell so – without frightful words,
Would he had killed him; 'twould have eased our
swords.
[Exeunt Vindice and Hippolito furtively]

DUKE   Be comforted, our duchess, he shall die.
[Exit Duchess]

LUSSURIOSO   Where's this slave-pander now? Out of
mine eye,   35
Guilty of this abuse.
Enter Spurio with his two Servants

SPURIO   Y'are villains, fablers!
You have knaves' chins and harlots' tongues; you lie,
And I will damn you with one meal a day.

FIRST SERVANT   O good my lord!
PURIO   'Sblood, you shall never sup.
SECOND SERVANT   O, I beseech you, sir!
PURIO   To let my sword   40
  Catch cold so long, and miss him.
FIRST SERVANT   Troth, my lord,
  'Twas his intent to meet there.
PURIO   Heart, he's yonder!
  Ha, what news here? Is the day out o' th' socket,
  That it is noon at midnight? the court up?
  How comes the guard so saucy with his elbows?   45
USSURIOSO [*aside*]   The bastard here?
  Nay, then the truth of my intent shall out. –
  My lord and father, hear me.
DUKE   Bear him hence.
USSURIOSO   I can with loyalty excuse –
DUKE   Excuse? To prison with the villain!   50
  Death shall not long lag after him.
PURIO [*aside*]   Good, i' faith; then 'tis not much amiss.
USSURIOSO   Brothers, my best release lies on your
      tongues;
  I pray persuade for me.
MBITIOSO   It is our duties;
  Make yourself sure of us.
UPERVACUO   We'll sweat in pleading.   55
USSURIOSO   And I may live to thank you.
      Exeunt [*Lussurioso and Guards*]
MBITIOSO   [*aside*]   No, thy death
  Shall thank me better.
PURIO   [*aside*]   He's gone; I'll after him,
  And know his trespass, seem to bear a part
  In all his ills, but with a Puritan heart.
      Exit [*Spurio*]
MBITIOSO   [*aside to Supervacuo*]

Now, brother, let our hate and love be woven   6o
So subtly together, that in speaking
One word for his life, we may make three for his death.
The craftiest pleader gets most gold for breath.
SUPERVACUO [*aside to Ambitioso*]   Set on; I'll not be far
    behind you, brother.
DUKE   Is't possible a son should be disobedient as far
    as the sword?   6
    It is the highest; he can go no farther.
AMBITIOSO   My gracious lord, take pity –
DUKE   Pity, boys?
AMBITIOSO   Nay, we'd be loath to move your grace too
    much.
    We know the trespass is unpardonable,
    Black, wicked, and unnatural.   7
SUPERVACUO   In a son, O monstrous!
AMBITIOSO   Yet, my lord,
    A duke's soft hand strokes the rough head of law,
    And makes it lie smooth.
DUKE   But my hand shall ne'er do 't.
AMBITIOSO   That as you please, my lord.
SUPERVACUO   We must needs confess
    Some father would have entered into hate   7
    So deadly pointed, that before his eyes
    He would ha' seen the execution sound,
    Without corrupted favor.
AMBITIOSO   But my lord,
    Your grace may live the wonder of all times,
    In pard'ning that offense which never yet   8
    Had face to beg a pardon.
DUKE   [*aside*]   Honey? How's this?
AMBITIOSO   Forgive him, good my lord; he's your own
    son,
    And I must needs say, 'twas the vilelier done.

SUPERVACUO   He's the next heir; yet this true reason
   gathers:
   None can possess that dispossess their fathers.   85
   Be merciful –
DUKE [*aside*]   Here's no stepmother's wit;
   I'll try 'em both upon their love and hate.
AMBITIOSO   Be merciful – although –
DUKE   You have prevailed.
   My wrath, like flaming wax, hath spent itself.
   I know 'twas but some peevish moon in him;   90
   Go, let him be released.
SUPERVACUO [*aside to Ambitioso*] 'Sfoot, how now,
   brother?
AMBITIOSO   Your grace doth please to speak beside
   your spleen;
   I would it were so happy.
DUKE   Why, go release him.
SUPERVACUO   O, my good lord, I know the fault's too
   weighty
   And full of general loathing; too inhuman,   95
   Rather by all men's voices worthy death.
DUKE   'Tis true too.
   Here then, receive this signet: doom shall pass.
   Direct it to the judges; he shall die
   Ere many days. Make haste.
AMBITIOSO   All speed that may be.   100
   We could have wished his burden not so sore;
   We knew your grace did but delay before.
      Exeunt [*Ambitioso and Supervacuo*]
DUKE   Here's envy with a poor thin cover o'er't,
   Like scarlet hid in lawn, easily spied through.
   This their ambition by the mother's side   105
   Is dangerous, and for safety must be purged.
   I will prevent their envies; sure it was

But some mistaken fury in our son,
Which these aspiring boys would climb upon.
He shall be released suddenly.   110
    Enter Nobles
FIRST NOBLE   Good morning to your grace.
DUKE   Welcome, my lords.
    [*Nobles kneel*]
SECOND NOBLE   Our knees shall take away
  The office of our feet forever,
  Unless your grace bestow a father's eye
  Upon the clouded fortunes of your son,   11
  And in compassionate virtue grant him that
  Which makes e'en mean men happy: liberty.
DUKE [*aside*]   How seriously their loves and honours woo
  For that which I am about to pray them do:
  Which – [*to the Nobles*] rise, my lords; your knees sign
    his release.   12
  We freely pardon him.
FIRST NOBLE   We owe your grace much thanks, and he
    much duty.
    Exeunt [*Nobles*]
DUKE   It well becomes that judge to nod at crimes
  That does commit greater himself, and lives.
  I may forgive a disobedient error   12
  That expect pardon for adultery
  And in my old days am a youth in lust.
  Many a beauty have I turned to poison
  In the denial, covetous of all.
  Age hot is like a monster to be seen: 13
  My hairs are white, and yet my sins are green.
    [*Exit*]

Act III Scene I

Enter Ambitioso and Supervacuo

SUPERVACUO   Brother, let my opinion sway you once;
  I speak it for the best, to have him die
  Surest and soonest. If the signet come
  Unto the judges' hands, why then his doom
  Will be deferred till sittings and court-days,   5
  Juries, and further. Faiths are bought and sold;
  Oaths in these days are but the skin of gold.
AMBITIOSO   In troth, 'tis true too!
SUPERVACUO   Then let's set by the judges
  And fall to the officers. 'Tis but mistaking
  The duke our father's meaning, and where he named   10
  'Ere many days', 'tis but forgetting that,
  And have him die i' th' morning.
AMBITIOSO   Excellent!
  Then am I heir – duke in a minute.
SUPERVACUO *[aside, grasping his sword]*   Nay,
  An he were once puffed out, here is a pin
  Should quickly prick your bladder.
AMBITIOSO   Blest occasion!   15
  He being packed, we'll have some trick and wile
  To wind our younger brother out of prison,
  That lies in for the rape: the lady's dead,
  And people's thought will soon be burièd.
SUPERVACUO   We may with safety do't, and live and
    feed;   20
  The duchess' sons are too proud to bleed.
AMBITIOSO   We are i'faith, to say true. Come, let's not
    linger.
  I'll to the officers; go you before,
  And set an edge upon the executioner.

SUPERVACUO   Let me alone to grind him.
AMBITIOSO   Meet; farewell. –   2⁵
    Exit [Supervacuo]
    I am next now; I rise just in that place
    Where thou'rt cut off – upon thy neck, kind brother.
    The falling of one head lifts up another.
        Exit

Act III Scene II

    Enter, with the Nobles, Lussurioso from prison
LUSSURIOSO   My lords,
    I am so much indebted to your loves
    For this, O this delivery.
FIRST NOBLE   But our duties,
    My lord, unto the hopes that grow in you.
LUSSURIOSO   If e'er I live to be myself, I'll thank you.
    O liberty, thou sweet and heavenly dame!
    But hell for prison is too mild a name.
        Exeunt

Act III Scene III

    Enter Ambitioso and Supervacuo, with Officers
AMBITIOSO   Officers, here's the duke's signet, your firm
        warrant,
    Brings the command of present death along with it
    Unto our brother, the duke's son. We are sorry
    That we are so unnaturally employed
    In such an unkind office, fitter far
    For enemies than brothers.

SUPERVACUO   But you know
  The duke's command must be obeyed.
FIRST OFFICER   It must and shall, my lord. This
      morning then,
  So suddenly?
AMBITIOSO   Aye, alas. Poor, good soul,
  He must breakfast betimes; the executioner   10
  Stands ready to put forth his cowardly valour.
SECOND OFFICER   Already?
SUPERVACUO   Already, i'faith. O sir, destruction hies,
  And that is least impudent, soonest dies.
FIRST OFFICER   Troth, you say true, my lord; we take
      our leaves.   15
  Our office shall be sound; we'll not delay
  The third part of a minute.
AMBITIOSO   Therein you show
  Yourselves good men, and upright officers.
  Pray let him die as private as he may;
  Do him that favour, for the gaping people   20
  Will but trouble him at his prayers
  And make him curse and swear, and so die black.
  Will you be so far kind?
FIRST OFFICER   It shall be done, my lord.
AMBITIOSO   Why, we do thank you; if we live to be,
  You shall have a better office.
SECOND OFFICER   Your good lordship.   25
SUPERVACUO   Commend us to the scaffold in our tears.
FIRST OFFICER   We'll weep, and do your commendations.
      Exeunt [Officers]
AMBITIOSO   Fine fools in office!
SUPERVACUO   Things fall out so fit!
AMBITIOSO   So happily! Come, brother, ere next clock
  His head will be made serve a bigger block.   30
      Exeunt

Act III Scene IV

Enter in prison Junior Brother

JUNIOR BROTHER Keeper!

[*Enter Keeper*]

KEEPER My lord.

JUNIOR BROTHER No news lately from our brothers? Are they unmindful of us?

KEEPER My lord, a messenger came newly in and brought this from 'em.

[*Gives him a letter*]

JUNIOR BROTHER Nothing but paper comforts? I looked for my delivery before this, had they been worth their oaths. Prithee, be from us.

[*Exit Keeper*]

Now, what say you, forsooth? Speak out, I pray. ([*Reading the*] *letter*) 'Brother, be of good cheer.' 'Slud, it begins like a whore, with good cheer. 'Thou shalt not be long a prisoner.' Not five-and-thirty year, like a bankrupt, I think so. 'We have thought upon a device to get thee out by a trick.' By a trick! Pox o' your trick, an it be so long a-playing. 'And so rest comforted, be merry and expect it suddenly.' Be merry! Hang merry! Draw and quarter merry! I'll be mad. [*Tears up the letter*] Is't not strange that a man should lie in a whole month for a woman? Well, we shall see how sudden our brothers will be in their promise. I must expect still a trick. I shall not be long a prisoner.

[*Enter Keeper*]

How now, what news?

KEEPER Bad news, my lord, I am discharged of you.

JUNIOR BROTHER Slave, call'st thou that bad news? I thank you, brothers.

KEEPER   My lord, 'twill prove so: here come the officers
   into whose hands I must commit you.
    [*Enter four Officers*]
JUNIOR BROTHER   Ha? Officers! what? why?   30
FIRST OFFICER   You must pardon us, my lord, our office
   Must be sound. Here is our warrant, the signet
   From the duke; you must straight suffer.
JUNIOR BROTHER   Suffer?
   I'll suffer you to be gone; I'll suffer you
   To come no more. What would you have me suffer?   35
SECOND OFFICER
   My lord, those words were better changed to prayers.
   The time's but brief with you; prepare to die.
JUNIOR BROTHER   Sure 'tis not so.
THIRD OFFICER   It is too true, my lord.
JUNIOR BROTHER   I tell you 'tis not, for the duke my father
   Deferred me till next sitting, and I look   40
   E'en every minute, threescore times an hour,
   For a release, a trick wrought by my brothers.
FIRST OFFICER   A trick, my lord? If you expect such
    comfort,
   Your hope's as fruitless as a barren woman.
   Your brothers were the unhappy messengers   45
   That brought this powerful token for your death.
JUNIOR BROTHER   My brothers? No, no!
SECOND OFFICER   'Tis most true, my lord.
JUNIOR BROTHER   My brothers to bring a warrant for
   my death?
   How strange this shows!
THIRD OFFICER   There's no delaying time.
JUNIOR BROTHER   Desire 'em hither, call 'em up. My
    brothers?   50
   They shall deny it to your faces.
FIRST OFFICER   My lord,

They're far enough by this, at least at court,
And this most strict command they left behind 'em.
When grief swum in their eyes, they showed like
    brothers,
Brimful of heavy sorrow; but the duke   55
Must have his pleasure.

JUNIOR BROTHER   His pleasure!

FIRST OFFICER
These were their last words which my memory bears:
'Commend us to the scaffold in our tears.'

JUNIOR BROTHER   Pox dry their tears! What should I
    do with tears?
I hate 'em worse than any citizen's son   60
Can hate salt water. Here came a letter now,
New-bleeding from their pens, scarce stinted yet –
Would I'd been torn in pieces when I tore it.
    [*He picks up the pieces*]
Look, you officious whoresons, words of comfort:
'Not long a prisoner.'   65

FIRST OFFICER   It says true in that, sir, for you must suffer
presently.

JUNIOR BROTHER   A villainous duns upon the letter,
knavish exposition! Look you then here, sir: 'We'll get
thee out by a trick,' says he.   70

SECOND OFFICER   That may hold too, sir, for you know
a trick is commonly four cards, which was meant by
us four officers.

JUNIOR BROTHER   Worse and worse dealing.

FIRST OFFICER   The hour beckons us,
The headsman waits; lift up your eyes to heaven.   75

JUNIOR BROTHER
I thank you, faith; good, pretty, wholesome counsel!
I should look up to heaven as you said,
Whilst he behind me cozens me of my head.

Aye, that's the trick.

THIRD OFFICER   You delay too long, my lord.

JUNIOR BROTHER   Stay, good authority's bastards; since I must   80
    Through brothers' perjury die, O let me venom
    Their souls with curses.

FIRST OFFICER   Come, 'tis no time to curse.

JUNIOR BROTHER   Must I bleed then, without respect of sign?
    Well –
    My fault was sweet sport, which the world approves;   85
    I die for that which every woman loves.

    Exeunt

Act III Scene V

*Enter Vindice [disguised] with Hippolito, [who holds
a torch and an incense-burner]*

VINDICE   O sweet, delectable, rare, happy, ravishing!

HIPPOLITO   Why, what's the matter, brother?

VINDICE   O, 'tis able
    To make a man spring up, and knock his forehead
    Against yon silver ceiling.

HIPPOLITO   Prithee tell me,
    Why may not I partake with you? You vowed once   5
    To give me share to every tragic thought.

VINDICE   By th' mass, I think I did too;
    Then I'll divide it to thee. The old duke,
    Thinking my outward shape and inward heart
    Are cut out of one piece (for he that prates his secrets,   10
    His heart stands o' th' outside), hires me by price
    To greet him with a lady

In some fit place veiled from the eyes o' th' court,
Some darkened, blushless angle, that is guilty
Of his forefathers' lusts and great folks' riots;   15
To which I easily (to maintain my shape)
Consented, and did wish his impudent grace
To meet her here in this unsunnèd lodge,
Wherein 'tis night at noon; and here the rather
Because, unto the torturing of his soul,   20
The bastard and the duchess have appointed
Their meeting too in this luxurious circle,
Which most afflicting sight will kill his eyes
Before we kill the rest of him.

HIPPOLITO   'Twill, i'faith; most dreadfully digested.   25
  I see not how you could have missed me, brother.

VINDICE   True, but the violence of my joy forgot it.

HIPPOLITO   Aye, but where's that lady now?

VINDICE   O, at that word
  I'm lost again: you cannot find me yet.
  I'm in a throng of happy apprehensions.   30
  He's suited for a lady; I have took care
  For a delicious lip, a sparkling eye.
  You shall be witness, brother.
  Be ready; stand with your hat off.
        Exit [Vindice]

HIPPOLITO   Troth, I wonder what lady it should be?   35
  Yet 'tis no wonder, now I think again,
  To have a lady stoop to a duke, that stoops unto his
      men.
  'Tis common to be common, through the world:
  And there's more private-common shadowing vices
  Than those who are known both by their names and
      prices.   40
  'Tis part of my allegiance to stand bare
  To the duke's concubine – and here she comes.

Enter Vindice, with the skull of his love dressed up in
tires [and masked]
VINDICE [*to the skull*]   Madam, his grace will not be
   absent long. –
Secret? ne'er doubt us, madam.'Twill be worth
Three velvet gowns to your ladyship. – Known?   45
Few ladies respect that! – Disgrace? A poor thin shell;
'Tis the best grace you have to do it well.
I'll save your hand that labour; I'll unmask you!
   [*Vindice unmasks the skull*]
HIPPOLITO   Why, brother, brother!
VINDICE   Art thou beguiled now? Tut, a lady can,   50
At such all-hid, beguile a wiser man.
Have I not fitted the old surfeiter
With a quaint piece of beauty? Age and bare bone
Are e'er allied in action. Here's an eye
Able to tempt a great man – to serve God;   55
A pretty hanging lip, that has forgot now to dissemble;
Methinks this mouth should make a swearer tremble,
A drunkard clasp his teeth, and not undo 'em
To suffer wet damnation to run through 'em.
Here's a cheek keeps her colour, let the wind go whistle.   60
Spout, rain, we fear thee not; be hot or cold,
All's one with us. And is not he absurd,
Whose fortunes are upon their faces set,
That fear no other god but wind and wet?
HIPPOLITO   Brother, y'ave spoke that right.   65
Is this the form that, living, shone so bright?
VINDICE   The very same.
And now methinks I could e'en chide myself
For doting on her beauty, though her death
Shall be revenged after no common action.   70
Does the silkworm expend her yellow labours
For thee? for thee does she undo herself?

Are lordships sold to maintain ladyships
For the poor benefit of a bewitching minute?
Why does yon fellow falsify highways,   7⁵
And put his life between the judge's lips,
To refine such a thing, keeps horse and men
To beat their valours for her?
Surely we are all mad people, and they
Whom we think are, are not; we mistake those: 8⁰
'Tis we are mad in sense, they but in clothes.
HIPPOLITO   Faith, and in clothes too we, give us our due.
VINDICE   Does every proud and self-affecting dame
Camphor her face for this? and grieve her Maker
In sinful baths of milk, when many an infant starves,   8⁵
For her superfluous outside – all for this?
Who now bids twenty pound a night, prepares
Music, perfumes, and sweetmeats? All are hushed;
Thou may'st lie chaste now! It were fine, methinks,
To have thee seen at revels, forgetful feasts,   9⁰
And unclean brothels; sure, 'twould fright the sinner
And make him a good coward, put a reveller
Out of his antic amble,
And cloy an epicure with empty dishes.
Here might a scornful and ambitious woman   9⁵
Look through and through herself. See, ladies, with
    false forms
You deceive men, but cannot deceive worms.
Now to my tragic business. Look you, brother,
I have not fashioned this only for show
And useless property; no, it shall bear a part   10⁰
E'en in it own revenge. This very skull,
Whose mistress the duke poisoned with this drug,
The mortal curse of the earth, shall be revenged
In the like strain, and kiss his lips to death.
As much as the dumb thing can, he shall feel;   10⁵

What fails in poison, we'll supply in steel.

HIPPOLITO   Brother, I do applaud thy constant vengeance,
The quaintness of thy malice, above thought.

VINDICE   [*putting poison on the skull's mouth*]
So, 'tis laid on: now come and welcome, duke;
I have her for thee. I protest it, brother,   110
Methinks she makes almost as fair a sign
As some old gentlewoman in a periwig.
[*To the skull*] Hide thy face now for shame; thou hadst
    need have a mask now.
    [*Vindice puts the mask back on the skull*]
'Tis vain when beauty flows, but when it fleets,   115
This would become graves better than the streets.

HIPPOLITO   You have my voice in that.
    [*Noises within*]
                                    Hark, the duke's come.

VINDICE   Peace, let's observe what company he brings,
And how he does absent 'em; for you know
He'll wish all private. Brother, fall you back a little   120
With the bony lady.

HIPPOLITO   That I will.
    [*Hippolito retires with the skull and the torch*]

VINDICE   So, so –
Now nine years' vengeance crowd into a minute!
    [*Enter the Duke and Gentlemen; Vindice is unobserved*]

DUKE   You shall have leave to leave us, with this charge,
Upon your lives: if we be missed by th' duchess
Or any of the nobles, to give out   125
We're privately rid forth.

VINDICE   [*aside*]   O happiness!

DUKE   With some few honourable gentlemen, you may say;
You may name those that are away from court.

[FIRST] GENTLEMAN   Your will and pleasure shall be
    done, my lord.

[*Exeunt Gentlemen*]
VINDICE [*aside*]   'Privately rid forth!'   13
  He strives to make sure work on 't.
      [*Steps forward*]
                                        Your good grace.
DUKE   Piato, well done. Hast brought her? What lady is't?
VINDICE   Faith, my lord, a country lady, a little bashful
  at first, as most of them are, but after the first kiss, my
  lord, the worst is past with them. Your grace knows   13
  now what you have to do. Sh'as somewhat a grave
  look with her, but –
DUKE   I love that best. Conduct her.
VINDICE   [*aside*]   Have at all!
DUKE   In gravest looks the greatest faults seem less;
  Give me that sin that's robed in holiness.   14
VINDICE [*aside to Hippolito*]   Back with the torch,
      brother; raise the perfumes.
      [*Hippolito retires with the torch and lights the incense-
      burner. Vindice advances with the skull*]
DUKE   How sweet can a duke breathe? Age has no fault;
  Pleasure should meet in a perfumèd mist. –
  Lady, sweetly encountered. I came from court,
  I must be bold with you.
      [*Kisses the skull*]
                                  O, what's this! O!   14
VINDICE   Royal villain! white devil!
DUKE   O!
VINDICE   Brother,
  Place the torch here, that his affrighted eyeballs
  May start into those hollows. Duke, dost know
  Yon dreadful vizard? View it well; 'tis the skull
  Of Gloriana, whom thou poisonedst last.   15
DUKE   O, 't'as poisoned me.
VINDICE   Didst not know that till now?

DUKE   What are you two?

VINDICE   Villains all three.
  The very ragged bone has been sufficiently revenged.

DUKE   O Hippolito, call treason!

HIPPOLITO   Yes, my good lord: treason, treason, treason!   155
    Stamping on him

DUKE   Then I'm betrayed.

VINDICE   Alas, poor lecher, in the hands of knaves,
  A slavish duke is baser than his slaves.

DUKE   My teeth are eaten out.

VINDICE   Hadst any left?

HIPPOLITO   I think but few.

VINDICE   Then those that did eat are eaten.   160

DUKE   O, my tongue!

VINDICE   Your tongue? 'twill teach you to kiss closer,
  Not like a slobbering Dutchman. You have eyes still:
  Look, monster, what a lady hast thou made me
  My once-betrothèd wife.

DUKE   Is it thou, villain?   165
  Nay, then –

VINDICE   'Tis I, 'tis Vindice, 'tis I.

HIPPOLITO   And let this comfort thee: our lord and father
  Fell sick upon the infection of thy frowns
  And died in sadness; be that thy hope of life.

DUKE   O!

VINDICE   He had his tongue, yet grief made him die
    speechless.   170
  Puh, 'tis but early yet; now I'll begin
  To stick thy soul with ulcers. I will make
  Thy spirit grievous sore; it shall not rest,
  But like some pestilent man toss in thy breast.
  Mark me, duke: 175
  Thou'rt a renownèd, high, and mighty cuckold.

DUKE   O!

VINDICE   Thy bastard, thy bastard rides a-hunting in
    thy brow.
DUKE   Millions of deaths!
VINDICE   Nay, to afflict thee more,
  Here in this lodge they meet for damnèd clips;
  Those eyes shall see the incest of their lips.   180
DUKE   Is there a hell besides this, villains?
VINDICE   Villain!
  Nay, heaven is just, scorns are the hires of scorns;
  I ne'er knew yet adulterer without horns.
HIPPOLITO   Once ere they die 'tis quitted.
    [*Music within*]
VINDICE   Hark, the music;
  Their banquet is prepared, they're coming –   184
DUKE   O, kill me not with that sight.
VINDICE   Thou shalt not lose that sight for all thy
    dukedom.
DUKE   Traitors, murderers!
VINDICE   What, is not thy tongue eaten out yet?
  Then we'll invent a silence. Brother, stifle the torch.   190
    [*Hippolito puts out the torch*]
DUKE   Treason, murder!
VINDICE   Nay, faith, we'll have you hushed. – Now with
    thy dagger
  Nail down his tongue, and mine shall keep possession
  About his heart; if he but gasp, he dies.
  We dread not death to quittance injuries. Brother,   195
  If he but wink, not brooking the foul object,
  Let our two other hands tear up his lids
  And make his eyes like comets shine through blood:
  When the bad bleeds, then is the tragedy good.
HIPPOLITO   Whist, brother, music's at our ear; they come. 200

Enter Spurio meeting the Duchess [and Attendants with torches. Spurio and the Duchess kiss]

SPURIO   Had not that kiss a taste of sin, 'twere sweet.

DUCHESS   Why, there's no pleasure sweet but it is sinful.

SPURIO   True, such a bitter sweetness fate hath given,
Best side to us is the worst side to heaven.

DUCHESS   Push, come; 'tis the old duke thy doubtful father,   205
The thought of him rubs heaven in thy way.
But I protest, by yonder waxen fire,
Forget him, or I'll poison him.

SPURIO   Madam, you urge a thought which ne'er had life.
So deadly do I loathe him for my birth,   210
That if he took me hasped within his bed,
I would add murder to adultery,
And with my sword give up his years to death.

DUCHESS   Why, now thou'rt sociable; let's in and feast.
Loud'st music sound! Pleasure is banquet's guest.   215
Exeunt [Spurio and Duchess, with Attendants, as offstage music plays]

DUKE   I cannot brook –
[Vindice stabs the Duke to death]

VINDICE   The brook is turned to blood.

HIPPOLITO   Thanks to loud music.

VINDICE   'Twas our friend indeed.
'Tis state in music for a duke to bleed.
The dukedom wants a head, though yet unknown:
As fast as they peep up, let's cut 'em down.   220
Exeunt

Act III Scene VI

Enter Ambitioso and Supervacuo

AMBITIOSO   Was not his execution rarely plotted?
We are the duke's sons now.

SUPERVACUO   Aye, you may thank my policy for that.

AMBITIOSO   Your policy? For what?

SUPERVACUO   Why, was 't not my invention, brother,   5
To slip the judges? And, in lesser compass,
Did not I draw the model of his death,
Advising you to sudden officers,
And e'en extemporal execution?

AMBITIOSO   Heart, 'twas a thing I thought on too.   10

SUPERVACUO   You thought on't too! 'Sfoot, slander not
    your thoughts
With glorious untruth; I know 'twas from you.

AMBITIOSO   Sir, I say 'twas in my head.

SUPERVACUO   Aye, like your brains then:
Ne'er to come out as long as you lived.

AMBITIOSO   You'd have the honour on't, forsooth, that
    your wit   15
Led him to the scaffold.

SUPERVACUO   Since it is my due,
I'll publish't, but I'll ha't in spite of you.

AMBITIOSO   Methinks y'are much too bold; you should
    a little
Remember us, brother, next to be honest duke.

SUPERVACUO [*aside*]   Aye, it shall be as easy for you to
    be duke   20
As to be honest, and that's never, i'faith.

AMBITIOSO   Well, cold he is by this time; and because
We're both ambitious, be it our amity,
And let the glory be shared equally.

SUPERVACUO   I am content to that.   25

80

AMBITIOSO   This night our younger brother shall out of
    prison;
  I have a trick.
SUPERVACUO   A trick, prithee, what is't?
AMBITIOSO   We'll get him out by a wile.
SUPERVACUO   Prithee, what wile?
AMBITIOSO   No, sir, you shall not know it till't be done;
  For then you'd swear 'twere yours.   30
    [*Enter an Officer, with a head covered in a cloth*]
SUPERVACUO   How now! what's he?
AMBITIOSO   One of the officers.
SUPERVACUO   Desired news.
AMBITIOSO   How now, my friend?
OFFICER   My lords, under your pardon, I am allotted
  To that desertless office to present you
  With the yet bleeding head.
    [*Gives the covered head to Supervacuo*]
SUPERVACUO [*aside to Ambitioso*]   Ha, ha, excellent.   35
AMBITIOSO [*aside to Supervacuo*]   All's sure our own.
    Brother, canst weep, think'st thou?
  'Twould grace our flattery much. Think of some
    dame;
  'Twill teach thee to dissemble.
SUPERVACUO [*aside to Ambitioso*]   I have thought;
  Now for yourself.
AMBITIOSO [*aloud*]   Our sorrows are so fluent,
  Our eyes o'erflow our tongues; words spoke in tears   40
  Are like the murmurs of the waters; the sound
  Is loudly heard, but cannot be distinguished.
SUPERVACUO   How died he, pray?
OFFICER   O, full of rage and spleen.
SUPERVACUO   He died most valiantly then; we're glad
  To hear it.
OFFICER   We could not woo him once to pray.   45

AMBITIOSO   He showed himself a gentleman in that,
 Give him his due.
OFFICER   But in the stead of prayer,
 He drew forth oaths.
SUPERVACUO   Then did he pray, dear heart,
 Although you understood him not.
OFFICER   My lords,
 E'en at his last, with pardon be it spoke,   5(
 He cursed you both.
SUPERVACUO   He cursed us? 'las, good soul.
AMBITIOSO   It was not in our powers, but the duke's
     pleasure. –
 [*Aside*]   Finely dissembled o' both sides, sweet fate,
 O happy opportunity!
     Enter Lussurioso
LUSSURIOSO   Now, my lords –
BOTH   O!
LUSSURIOSO   Why do you shun me, brothers?   5(
 You may come nearer now;
 The savour of the prison has forsook me.
 I thank such kind lords as yourselves, I'm free.
AMBITIOSO   Alive!
SUPERVACUO   In health!
AMBITIOSO   Released?
 We were both e'en amazed with joy to see it.   6(
LUSSURIOSO   I am much to thank you.
SUPERVACUO   Faith, we spared no tongue unto my lord
     the duke.
AMBITIOSO   I know your delivery, brother,
 Had not been half so sudden but for us.
SUPERVACUO   O how we pleaded!
LUSSURIOSO   Most deserving brothers,   6(
 In my best studies I will think of it.
     Exit Lussurioso

AMBITIOSO   O death and vengeance!

SUPERVACUO   Hell and torments!

AMBITIOSO   Slave, cam'st thou to delude us?

OFFICER   Delude you, my lords?

SUPERVACUO   Aye, villain, where's this head now?

OFFICER   Why, here, my lord.
  Just after his delivery, you both came   70
  With warrant from the duke to behead your brother.

AMBITIOSO   Aye, our brother, the duke's son.

OFFICER   The duke's son,
  My lord, had his release before you came.

AMBITIOSO   Whose head's that then?

OFFICER   His whom you left command for,
  Your own brother's.

AMBITIOSO   Our brother's? O furies!   75

SUPERVACUO   Plagues!

AMBITIOSO   Confusions!

SUPERVACUO   Darkness!

AMBITIOSO   Devils!

SUPERVACUO   Fell it out so accursèdly?

AMBITIOSO   So damnedly?

SUPERVACUO   [*brandishing the head*]
  Villain, I'll brain thee with it.

OFFICER   O my good lord!

SUPERVACUO   The devil overtake thee!
    [*Exit Officer*]

AMBITIOSO   O, fatal!

SUPERVACUO   O prodigious to our bloods.

AMBITIOSO   Did we dissemble?   80

SUPERVACUO   Did we make our tears women for thee?

AMBITIOSO   Laugh and rejoice for thee?

SUPERVACUO   Bring warrant for thy death?

AMBITIOSO   Mock off thy head?

SUPERVACUO   You had a trick, you had a wile, forsooth.

AMBITIOSO A murrain meet 'em! There's none of 85
these wiles that ever come to good. I see now there is
nothing sure in mortality, but mortality.
Well, no more words; shalt be revenged, i' faith.
Come, throw off clouds now, brother; think of
vengeance
And deeper-settled hate. Sirrah, sit fast, 90
We'll pull down all, but thou shalt down at last.
Exeunt, [carrying the head]

Act IV Scene I

Enter Lussurioso with Hippolito

LUSSURIOSO   Hippolito.

HIPPOLITO   My lord, has your good lordship
  Aught to command me in?

LUSSURIOSO   I prithee leave us.

HIPPOLITO [*aside*]   How's this? Come and leave us?

LUSSURIOSO   Hippolito.

HIPPOLITO   Your honour, I stand ready for any duteous
  employment.

LUSSURIOSO   Heart, what mak'st thou here?

HIPPOLITO   [*aside*]   A pretty lordly humour: 5
  He bids me to be present, to depart; something
  Has stung his honour.

LUSSURIOSO   Be nearer, draw nearer.
  Y'are not so good, methinks; I'm angry with you.

HIPPOLITO   With me, my lord? I'm angry with myself
  for't.

LUSSURIOSO   You did prefer a goodly fellow to me;   10
  'Twas wittily elected, 'twas. I thought
  H'ad been a villain, and he proves a knave,
  To me a knave.

HIPPOLITO   I chose him for the best, my lord.
  'Tis much my sorrow, if neglect in him
  Breed discontent in you.

LUSSURIOSO   Neglect! 'Twas will.   15
  Judge of it:
  Firmly to tell of an incredible act,
  Not to be thought, less to be spoken of,
  'Twixt my stepmother and the bastard, O,
  Incestuous sweets between 'em.

HIPPOLITO   Fie, my lord.   20

LUSSURIOSO   I in kind loyalty to my father's forehead
  Made this a desperate arm, and in that fury
  Committed treason on the lawful bed,
  And with my sword e'en rased my father's bosom,
  For which I was within a stroke of death.   2⁵
HIPPOLITO   Alack, I'm sorry.
      Enter Vindice
  [*Aside*]   'Sfoot, just upon the stroke
  Jars in my brother: 'twill be villainous music.
VINDICE   My honoured lord.
LUSSURIOSO   Away, prithee forsake us; hereafter we'll
    not know thee.
VINDICE   Not know me, my lord? Your lordship cannot
    choose.   3⁰
LUSSURIOSO   Begone, I say; thou art a false knave.
VINDICE   Why, the easier to be known, my lord.
LUSSURIOSO   Push, I shall prove too bitter with a
    word,
  Make thee a perpetual prisoner,
  And lay this iron-age upon thee.
VINDICE   [*aside*]   Mum!   3⁵
  For there's a doom would make a woman dumb.
  Missing the bastard, next him, the wind's come about;
  Now 'tis my brother's turn to stay, mine to go out.
      Exit Vindice
LUSSURIOSO   H'as greatly moved me.
HIPPOLITO   Much to blame, i' faith.
LUSSURIOSO   But I'll recover, to his ruin. 'Twas told me
    lately,   4⁰
  I know not whether falsely, that you'd a brother.
HIPPOLITO   Who, I? Yes, my good lord, I have a brother.
LUSSURIOSO   How chance the court ne'er saw him? Of
    what nature?
  How does he apply his hours?

HIPPOLITO   Faith, to curse fates
  Who, as he thinks, ordained him to be poor;   45
  Keeps at home, full of want and discontent.
LUSSURIOSO   There's hope in him, for discontent and
        want
  Is the best clay to mould a villain of.
  Hippolito, wish him repair to us.
  If there be aught in him to please our blood,   50
  For thy sake we'll advance him, and build fair
  His meanest fortunes; for it is in us
  To rear up towers from cottages.
HIPPOLITO   It is so, my lord. He will attend your honour;
  But he's a man in whom much melancholy dwells.   55
LUSSURIOSO   Why, the better; bring him to court.
HIPPOLITO   With willingness and speed.
  [*Aside*] Whom he cast off e'en now, must now succeed.
  Brother, disguise must off;
  In thine own shape now I'll prefer thee to him: 60
  How strangely does himself work to undo him.
        Exit [*Hippolito*]
LUSSURIOSO   This fellow will come fitly; he shall kill
  That other slave, that did abuse my spleen
  And made it swell to treason. I have put
  Much of my heart into him; he must die.   65
  He that knows great men's secrets and proves slight,
  That man ne'er lives to see his beard turn white.
  Aye, he shall speed him. I'll employ thee, brother:
  Slaves are but nails to drive out one another.
  He being of black condition, suitable   70
  To want and ill content, hope of preferment
  Will grind him to an edge.
        The Nobles enter
FIRST NOBLE   Good days unto your honour.
LUSSURIOSO   My kind lords, I do return the like.

87

SECOND NOBLE   Saw you my lord the duke?
LUSSURIOSO   My lord and father,   7
  Is he from court?
FIRST NOBLE   He's sure from court,
  But where, which way, his pleasure took we know not,
  Nor can we hear on 't.
    [*Enter the Duke's Gentlemen*]
LUSSURIOSO   Here come those should tell.
  Saw you my lord and father?
[FIRST] GENTLEMAN   Not since two hours before noon,
    my lord.   8
  And then he privately rid forth.
LUSSURIOSO   O, he's rode forth.
FIRST NOBLE   'Twas wondrous privately.
SECOND NOBLE   There's none i' th' court had any
    knowledge on't.
LUSSURIOSO   His grace is old and sudden; 'tis no treason
  To say, the duke my father has a humour,   8
  Or such a toy about him; what in us
  Would appear light, in him seems virtuous.
[FIRST] GENTLEMAN   'Tis oracle, my lord.
    Exeunt

Act IV Scene II

  Enter Vindice and Hippolito, Vindice out of his disguise
HIPPOLITO   So, so, all's as it should be; y'are yourself.
VINDICE   How that great villain puts me to my shifts.
HIPPOLITO   He that did lately in disguise reject thee
  Shall, now thou art thyself, as much respect thee.
VINDICE   'Twill be the quainter fallacy. But brother,
  'Sfoot, what use will he put me to now, think'st thou?

HIPPOLITO   Nay, you must pardon me in that, I know not.
   H'as some employment for you, but what 'tis
   He and his secretary the devil knows best.
VINDICE   Well, I must suit my tongue to his desires,   10
   What colour soe'er they be, hoping at last
   To pile up all my wishes on his breast.
HIPPOLITO   Faith, brother, he himself shows the way.
VINDICE   Now the duke is dead, the realm is clad in
    clay.
   His death being not yet known, under his name   15
   The people still are governed. Well, thou his son
   Art not long-lived; thou shalt not joy his death.
   To kill thee, then, I should most honour thee:
   For 'twould stand firm in every man's belief,
   Thou'st a kind child, and only died'st with grief.   20
HIPPOLITO   You fetch about well, but let's talk in
    present.
   How will you appear in fashion different,
   As well as in apparel, to make all things possible?
   If you be but once tripped, we fall forever.
   It is not the least policy to be doubtful;   25
   You must change tongue – familiar was your first.
VINDICE   Why, I'll bear me in some strain of melancholy,
   And string myself with heavy-sounding wire,
   Like such an instrument that speaks merry things
    sadly.
HIPPOLITO   Then 'tis as I meant;   30
   I gave you out at first in discontent.
VINDICE   I'll turn myself, and then –
    [*Enter Lussurioso*]
HIPPOLITO   'Sfoot, here he comes;
   Hast thought upon't?
VINDICE   Salute him, fear not me.
LUSSURIOSO   Hippolito.

HIPPOLITO   Your lordship.
LUSSURIOSO   What's he yonder?
HIPPOLITO   'Tis Vindice, my discontented brother,   35
   Whom, 'cording to your will, I've brought to court.
LUSSURIOSO   Is that thy brother? Beshrew me, a good
    presence.
   I wonder h'as been from the court so long!
   Come nearer.
HIPPOLITO   Brother, Lord Lussurioso, the duke's son.   40
LUSSURIOSO   Be more near to us. Welcome; nearer yet.
    [*Vindice*] *snatches off his hat and makes legs to him.*
    [*Hippolito stands apart*]
VINDICE   How don you? God you god den.
LUSSURIOSO   We thank thee.
   How strangely such a coarse, homely salute
   Shows in the palace, where we greet in fire:
   Nimble and desperate tongues, should we name   45
   God in a salutation, 'twould ne'er be stood on't –
    heaven!
   Tell me, what has made thee so melancholy?
VINDICE   Why, going to law.
LUSSURIOSO   Why, will that make a man melancholy?
VINDICE   Yes, to look long upon ink and black buckram.   50
   I went me to law in *anno quadragesimo secundo*, and I
   waded out of it in *anno sextagesimo tertio*.
LUSSURIOSO   What, three and twenty years in law?
VINDICE   I have known those that have been five and
   fifty, and all about pullen and pigs.   55
LUSSURIOSO   May it be possible such men should
    breathe,
   To vex the terms so much?
VINDICE   'Tis food to some, my lord.
   There are old men at the present, that are so poisoned
   with the affectation of law words (having had many

suits canvassed), that their common talk is nothing 60
but Barbary Latin. They cannot so much as pray but
in law, that their sins may be removed with a writ of
error, and their souls fetched up to heaven with a
sasarara.

LUSSURIOSO] It seems most strange to me; 65
Yet all the world meets round in the same bent:
Where the heart's set, there goes the tongue's consent.
How dost apply thy studies, fellow?

VINDICE Study? Why, to think how a great rich man
lies a-dying, and a poor cobbler tolls the bell for him; 70
how he cannot depart the world and see the great
chest stand before him; when he lies speechless, how
he will point you readily to all the boxes; and when he
is past all memory, as the gossips guess, then thinks he
of forfeitures and obligations. Nay, when to all men's 75
hearings he whurls and rattles in the throat, he's busy
threatening his poor tenants. And this would last me
now some seven years' thinking or thereabouts. But I
have a conceit a-coming in picture upon this: I draw it
myself, which, i' faith la, I'll present to your honour. 80
You shall not choose but like it, for your lordship
shall give me nothing for it.

USSURIOSO Nay, you mistake me then,
For I am published bountiful enough.
Let's taste of your conceit. 85

INDICE In picture, my lord?

USSURIOSO Aye, in picture.

INDICE Marry, this it is – *A usuring father, to be boiling
in hell, and his son and heir with a whore dancing over
him.*

IPPOLITO [*aside*] H'as pared him to the quick. 90

USSURIOSO The conceit's pretty, i' faith. But take't
upon my life, 'twill ne'er be liked.

VINDICE   No? Why, I'm sure the whore will be liked well
     enough.
HIPPOLITO [*aside*]   Aye, if she were out o' th' picture,   95
     he'd like her then himself.
VINDICE   And as for the son and heir, he shall be an
     eyesore to no young revellers, for he shall be drawn in
     cloth-of-gold breeches.
LUSSURIOSO   And thou hast put my meaning in the
     pockets,   100
     And canst not draw that out. My thought was this:
     To see the picture of a usuring father
     Boiling in hell, our rich men would ne'er like it.
VINDICE   O true, I cry you heartily mercy. I know the
     reason, for some of 'em had rather be damned indeed   105
     than damned in colours.
LUSSURIOSO [*aside*]   A parlous melancholy! H'as wit
     enough
     To murder any man, and I'll give him means.
     [*To Vindice*] I think thou art ill-monied?
VINDICE   Money! ho, ho,
     'T'as been my want so long, 'tis now my scoff;   110
     I've e'en forgot what colour silver's of.
LUSSURIOSO [*aside*]   It hits as I could wish.
VINDICE   I get good clothes
     Of those that dread my humour, and for table-room
     I feed on those that cannot be rid of me.
LUSSURIOSO   Somewhat to set thee up withal.   11
     [*He gives him gold*]
VINDICE   O, mine eyes!
LUSSURIOSO   How now, man?
VINDICE   Almost struck blind:
     This bright unusual shine to me seems proud;
     I dare not look till the sun be in a cloud.
LUSSURIOSO [*aside*]   I think I shall affect his melancholy. –

How are they now?

INDICE   The better for your asking.   120

USSURIOSO   You shall be better yet if you but fasten
  Truly on my intent. Now y'are both present,
  I will unbrace such a close, private villain
  Unto your vengeful swords, the like ne'er heard of,
  Who hath disgraced you much and injured us.   125

IPPOLITO   Disgraced us, my lord?

USSURIOSO   Aye, Hippolito.
  I kept it here till now, that both your angers
  Might meet him at once.

INDICE   I'm covetous
  To know the villain.

USSURIOSO [*to Hippolito*]   You know him – that slave
    pander
  Piato, whom we threatened last   130
  With irons in perpetual prisonment.

INDICE [*aside*]   All this is I.

IPPOLITO   Is't he, my lord?

USSURIOSO   I'll tell you;
  You first preferred him to me.

INDICE   Did you, brother?

IPPOLITO   I did indeed.

USSURIOSO   And the ingrateful villain,
  To quit that kindness, strongly wrought with me,   135
  Being, as you see, a likely man for pleasure,
  With jewels to corrupt your virgin sister.

IPPOLITO   O villain!

INDICE   He shall surely die that did it.

USSURIOSO   I, far from thinking any virgin harm,
  Especially knowing her to be as chaste   140
  As that part which scarce suffers to be touched,
  The eye, would not endure him.

INDICE   Would you not, my lord?

'Twas wondrous honourably done.

LUSSURIOSO But with some fine frowns kept him
    out.

VINDICE   Out, slave!

LUSSURIOSO What did me he but, in revenge of that,   14
    Went of his own free will to make infirm
    Your sister's honour, whom I honour with my soul
    For chaste respect; and not prevailing there
    (As 'twas but desperate folly to attempt it),
    In mere spleen, by the way, waylays your mother,   15
    Whose honour being a coward, as it seems,
    Yielded by little force.

VINDICE   Coward indeed.

LUSSURIOSO He, proud of their advantage (as he thought),
    Brought me these news for happy; but I, heaven
    Forgive me for't –

VINDICE   What did your honour?   15

LUSSURIOSO In rage pushed him from me,
    Trampled beneath his throat, spurned him, and bruised.
    Indeed, I was too cruel, to say troth.

HIPPOLITO Most nobly managed!

VINDICE [*aside*] Has not heaven an ear? Is all the lightning
    wasted?   16

LUSSURIOSO If I now were so impatient in a modest cause,
    What should you be?

VINDICE Full mad; he shall not live to see the moon
    change.

LUSSURIOSO He's about the palace. Hippolito, entice him
    this way, that thy brother may take full mark of him.   16

HIPPOLITO Heart! that shall not need, my lord; I can
    direct him so far.

LUSSURIOSO Yet for my hate's sake, go, wind him this
    way; I'll see him bleed myself.

HIPPOLITO [*aside to Vindice*] What now, brother?   17

VINDICE [*aside to Hippolito*]   Nay, e'en what you will;
   y'are put to't, brother!
HIPPOLITO [*aside*]   An impossible task, I'll swear,
   To bring him hither that's already here.
      Exit Hippolito
LUSSURIOSO   Thy name? I have forgot it.
VINDICE   Vindice, my lord.   175
LUSSURIOSO   'Tis a good name that.
VINDICE   Aye, a revenger.
LUSSURIOSO   It does betoken courage; thou shouldst
      be valiant
   And kill thine enemies.
VINDICE   That's my hope, my lord.
LUSSURIOSO   This slave is one.
VINDICE   I'll doom him.
LUSSURIOSO   Then I'll praise thee.
   Do thou observe me best, and I'll best raise thee.   180
      Enter Hippolito
VINDICE   Indeed, I thank you.
LUSSURIOSO   Now, Hippolito, where's the slave pander?
HIPPOLITO   Your good lordship
   Would have a loathsome sight of him, much offensive.
   He's not in case now to be seen, my lord;   185
   The worst of all the deadly sins is in him –
   That beggarly damnation, drunkenness.
LUSSURIOSO   Then he's a double slave.
VINDICE   [*aside*]   'Twas well conveyed,
   Upon a sudden wit.
LUSSURIOSO   What, are you both
   Firmly resolved? I'll see him dead myself.   190
VINDICE   Or else let not us live.
LUSSURIOSO   You may direct
   Your brother to take note of him.
HIPPOLITO   I shall.

LUSSURIOSO   Rise but in this, and you shall never fall.
VINDICE   Your honour's vassals.
LUSSURIOSO   [*aside*]   This was wisely carried.
　Deep policy in us makes fools of such:　　　　　　19
　Then must a slave die when he knows too much.
　　Exit Lussurioso
VINDICE   O, thou almighty patience! 'Tis my wonder
　That such a fellow, impudent and wicked,
　Should not be cloven as he stood,
　Or with a secret wind burst open!　　　　　　　20
　Is there no thunder left, or is't kept up
　In stock for heavier vengeance?
　　[*Thunder*]
　　　　　　　　　　　　There it goes!
HIPPOLITO   Brother, we lose ourselves.
VINDICE   　　　　　　　But I have found it.
　'Twill hold, 'tis sure; thanks, thanks to any spirit
　That mingled it 'mongst my inventions.　　　　　20
HIPPOLITO   What is't?
VINDICE   'Tis sound, and good; thou shalt partake it.
　I'm hired to kill myself.
HIPPOLITO   　　　　　True.
VINDICE   　　　　　　Prithee mark it.
　And the old duke being dead, but not conveyed;
　For he's already missed too, and you know
　Murder will peep out of the closest husk –　　　　21
HIPPOLITO   Most true.
VINDICE   　　　　　What say you then to this device?
　If we dressed up the body of the duke –
HIPPOLITO   In that disguise of yours.
VINDICE   　　　　　Y'are quick, y'ave reached it.
HIPPOLITO   I like it wondrously.
VINDICE   And being in drink, as you have published
　him,　　　　　　　　　　　　　　　　　21

To lean him on his elbow, as if sleep had caught him,
Which claims most interest in such sluggy men.
HIPPOLITO   Good yet, but here's a doubt:
We – thought by th'duke's son to kill that pander –
Shall, when he is known, be thought to kill the duke.   220
VINDICE   Neither – O thanks – it is substantial:
For that disguise being on him which I wore, it will
be thought I, which he calls the pander, did kill the
duke and fled away in his apparel, leaving him so
disguised to avoid swift pursuit.   225
HIPPOLITO   Firmer and firmer.
VINDICE   Nay, doubt not 'tis in grain;
I warrant it hold colour.
HIPPOLITO   Let's about it.
VINDICE   But by the way too, now I think on 't, brother,
Let's conjure that base devil out of our mother.
    Exeunt

Act IV Scene III

Enter the Duchess arm in arm with Spurio; he
seemeth lasciviously to her. After them, enter
Supervacuo, running with a rapier; Ambitioso stops
him

SPURIO   Madam, unlock yourself; should it be seen,
Your arm would be suspected.
DUCHESS   Who is't that dares suspect or this or these?
May not we deal our favours where we please?
SPURIO   I'm confident you may.
    Exeunt [Spurio and Duchess]
AMBITIOSO   'Sfoot, brother, hold.   5
SUPERVACUO   Wouldst let the bastard shame us?

97

AMBITIOSO   Hold, hold, brother!
   There's fitter time than now.
SUPERVACUO   Now, when I see it.
AMBITIOSO   'Tis too much seen already.
SUPERVACUO   Seen and known.
   The nobler she's, the baser is she grown.
AMBITIOSO   If she were bent lasciviously, the fault   10
   Of mighty women that sleep soft – O death!
   Must she needs choose such an unequal sinner,
   To make all worse?
SUPERVACUO   A bastard, the duke's bastard!
   Shame heaped on shame!
AMBITIOSO   O our disgrace!
   Most women have small waist the world throughout;   15
   But their desires are thousand miles about.
SUPERVACUO   Come, stay not here; let's after and prevent;
   Or else they'll sin faster than we'll repent.
      Exeunt

Act IV Scene IV

   Enter Vindice and Hippolito bringing out Gratiana,
   one by one shoulder, and the other by the other, with
   daggers in their hands
VINDICE   O thou, for whom no name is bad enough!
GRATIANA   What means my sons? What, will you murder
   me?
VINDICE   Wicked, unnatural parent!
HIPPOLITO   Fiend of women!
GRATIANA   O, are sons turned monsters? Help!
VINDICE   In vain.
GRATIANA   Are you so barbarous to set iron nipples   5

Upon the breast that gave you suck?

VINDICE   That breast
  Is turned to quarled poison.

GRATIANA   Cut not your days for 't; am not I your
    mother?

VINDICE   Thou dost usurp that tide now by fraud,
  For in that shell of mother breeds a bawd.   10

GRATIANA   A bawd! O name far loathsomer than hell!

HIPPOLITO   It should be so, knew'st thou thy office well.

GRATIANA   I hate it.

VINDICE   Ah, is 't possible, you powers on high,
  That women should dissemble when they die?   15

GRATIANA   Dissemble?

VINDICE   Did not the duke's son direct
  A fellow of the world's condition hither
  That did corrupt all that was good in thee?
  Made thee uncivilly forget thyself,
  And work our sister to his lust?

GRATIANA   Who, I?   20
  That had been monstrous! I defy that man
  For any such intent. None lives so pure,
  But shall be soiled with slander.
  Good son, believe it not.

VINDICE   O I'm in doubt
  Whether I'm myself or no.   25
  Stay, let me look again upon this face.
  Who shall be saved when mothers have no grace?

HIPPOLITO   'Twould make one half despair.

VINDICE   I was the man.
  Defy me now! Let's see; do 't modestly.

GRATIANA   O hell unto my soul!   30

VINDICE   In that disguise, I, sent from the duke's son,
  Tried you, and found you base metal,
  As any villain might have done.

GRATIANA O no,
No tongue but yours could have bewitched me so.
VINDICE   O nimble in damnation, quick in tune,   3⁵
There is no devil could strike fire so soon.
I am confuted in a word.
GRATIANA   O sons, forgive me! To myself I'll prove more
true;
You that should honour me, I kneel to you.
    [*Gratiana kneels, weeping*]
VINDICE   A mother to give aim to her own daughter!   4⁰
HIPPOLITO   True, brother; how far beyond nature 'tis,
Though many mothers do't.
VINDICE   Nay, an you draw tears once, go you to bed.
    [*Sheaths his dagger*]
Wet will make iron blush and change to red.
Brother, it rains; 'twill spoil your dagger; house it.   4⁵
HIPPOLITO [*puts away his dagger*]   'Tis done.
VINDICE   I'faith, 'tis a sweet shower; it does much good:
The fruitful grounds and meadows of her soul
Has been long dry. Pour down, thou blessèd dew.
Rise, mother. Troth, this shower has made you higher.   5⁰
GRATIANA   O you heavens,
Take this infectious spot out of my soul;
I'll rinse it in seven waters of mine eyes.
Make my tears salt enough to taste of grace!
To weep is to our sex naturally given;   5⁵
But to weep truly, that's a gift from heaven.
VINDICE   Nay, I'll kiss you now. Kiss her, brother!
Let's marry her to our souls, wherein's no lust,
And honourably love her.
HIPPOLITO   Let it be.
VINDICE   For honest women are so seld and rare,   6⁰
'Tis good to cherish those poor few that are.
O you of easy wax, do but imagine,

Now the disease has left you, how leprously
That office would have clinged unto your forehead.
All mothers that had any graceful hue   65
Would have worn masks to hide their face at you.
It would have grown to this: at your foul name
Green-coloured maids would have turned red with
    shame.

HIPPOLITO   And then our sister, full of hire and baseness.

VINDICE   There had been boiling lead again.   70
    The duke's son's great concubine!
    A drab of state, a cloth-o'-silver slut,
    To have her train borne up, and her soul trail i' th' dirt.
    Great –

HIPPOLITO   To be miserably great; rich, to be
    Eternally wretched.

VINDICE   O common madness!   75
    Ask but the thriving'st harlot in cold blood:
    She'd give the world to make her honour good.
    Perhaps you'll say, 'But only to th' duke's son,
    In private'. Why, she first begins with one,
    Who afterward to thousand proves a whore: 80
    'Break ice in one place, it will crack in more.'

GRATIANA   Most certainly applied!

HIPPOLITO   O brother, you forget our business.

VINDICE   And well remembered. Joy's a subtle elf;
    I think man's happiest when he forgets himself.   85
    Farewell, once dried, now holy-watered mead;
    Our hearts wear feathers that before wore lead.

GRATIANA   I'll give you this: that one I never knew
    Plead better for, and 'gainst, the devil than you.

VINDICE   You make me proud on 't.   90

HIPPOLITO   Commend us in all virtue to our sister.

VINDICE   Aye, for the love of heaven, to that true maid.

GRATIANA   With my best words.

VINDICE   Why, that was motherly said.
    Exeunt [Vindice and Hippolito]
GRATIANA   I wonder now what fury did transport me!
  I feel good thoughts begin to settle in me.   95
  O, with what forehead can I look on her,
  Whose honour I've so impiously beset!
    [Enter Castiza]
  And here she comes.
CASTIZA   Now, mother, you have wrought with me so
    strongly,
  That what for my advancement, as to calm   100
  The trouble of your tongue, I am content.
GRATIANA   Content, to what?
CASTIZA   To do as you have wished me:
  To prostitute my breast to the duke's son,
  And put myself to common usury.
GRATIANA   I hope you will not so.
CASTIZA   Hope you I will not?   105
  That's not the hope you look to be saved in.
GRATIANA   Truth, but it is.
CASTIZA   Do not deceive yourself;
  I am as you e'en out of marble wrought.
  What would you now? Are ye not pleased yet with me?
  You shall not wish me to be more lascivious   110
  Than I intend to be.
GRATIANA   Strike not me cold.
CASTIZA   How often have you charged me on your
    blessing
  To be a cursèd woman? When you knew
  Your blessing had no force to make me lewd,
  You laid your curse upon me; that did more.   115
  The mother's curse is heavy: where that fights,
  Sons set in storm, and daughters lose their lights.
GRATIANA   Good child, dear maid, if there be any spark

Of heavenly intellectual fire within thee,
O, let my breath revive it to a flame.   120
Put not all out with woman's wilful follies.
I am recovered of that foul disease
That haunts too many mothers; kind, forgive me,
Make me not sick in health. If then
My words prevailed when they were wickedness,   125
How much more now when they are just and good!

CASTIZA   I wonder what you mean. Are not you she
For whose infect persuasions I could scarce
Kneel out my prayers, and had much ado,
In three hours' reading, to untwist so much   130
Of the black serpent as you wound about me?

GRATIANA   'Tis unfruitful, held tedious, to repeat what's
    past.
I'm now your present mother.

CASTIZA   Push, now 'tis too late.

GRATIANA   Bethink again, thou know'st not what thou
    say'st.

CASTIZA   No? 'Deny advancement, treasure, the duke's
    son?'   135

GRATIANA   O see, I spoke those words, and now they
    poison me.
What will the deed do then?
Advancement? True, as high as shame can pitch.
For treasure – who e'er knew a harlot rich,
Or could build by the purchase of her sin   140
An hospital to keep their bastards in?
The duke's son? O, when women are young courtiers,
They are sure to be old beggars.
To know the miseries most harlots taste,
Thou'dst wish thyself unborn, when thou'rt unchaste. 145

CASTIZA   O mother, let me twine about your neck,
And kiss you till my soul melt on your lips.

I did but this to try you.

GRATIANA   O speak truth!

CASTIZA   Indeed, I did not;
   For no tongue has force to alter me from honest.   150
   If maidens would, men's words could have no power;
   A virgin honour is a crystal tower,
   Which, being weak, is guarded with good spirits;
   Until she basely yields, no ill inherits.

GRATIANA   O happy child! Faith and thy birth hath saved
    me.   155
   'Mongst thousand daughters, happiest of all others,
   Be thou a glass for maids, and I for mothers.
    Exeunt

Act V Scene I

Enter Vindice and Hippolito [with the Duke's body dressed in Vindice's disguise. They arrange the body to look like a sleeping man]

VINDICE   So, so, he leans well; take heed you wake him not, brother.

HIPPOLITO   I warrant you, my life for yours.

VINDICE   That's a good lay, for I must kill myself. Brother, that's I; that sits for me; do you mark it? And   5
I must stand ready here to make away myself yonder. I must sit to be killed, and stand to kill myself. I could vary it not so little as thrice over again; 't'as some eight returns, like Michaelmas term.

HIPPOLITO   That's enow, o' conscience.   10

VINDICE   But, sirrah, does the duke's son come single?

HIPPOLITO   No, there's the hell on 't. His faith's too feeble to go alone. He brings flesh-flies after him that will buzz against supper-time, and hum for his coming out.

VINDICE   Ah, the fly-flop of vengeance beat 'em to   15
pieces! Here was the sweetest occasion, the fittest hour, to have made my revenge familiar with him, show him the body of the duke his father, and how quaintly he died, like a politician, in hugger-mugger, made no man acquainted with it, and in catastrophe,   20
slain him over his father's breast, and – O I'm mad to lose such a sweet opportunity.

HIPPOLITO   Nay, push, prithee be content; there's no remedy present. May not hereafter times open in as fair faces as this?   25

VINDICE   They may, if they can paint so well.

HIPPOLITO   Come, now to avoid all suspicion, let's forsake this room, and be going to meet the duke's son.

VINDICE Content, I'm for any weather. Heart, step close;
    here he comes.   30
    Enter Lussurioso

HIPPOLITO My honoured lord!

LUSSURIOSO O me! you both present!

VINDICE E'en newly, my lord, just as your lordship
    entered now. About this place we had notice given he
    should be, but in some loathsome plight or other.   35

HIPPOLITO Came your honour private?

LUSSURIOSO Private enough for this; only a few attend
    my coming out.

HIPPOLITO [*aside*] Death rot those few.

LUSSURIOSO Stay, yonder's the slave.   40

VINDICE Mass, there's the slave indeed, my lord.
    [*Aside*] 'Tis a good child; he calls his father slave.

LUSSURIOSO Aye, that's the villain, the damned villain.
    Softly, tread easy.

VINDICE Puh, I warrant you, my lord, we'll stifle in our   45
    breaths.

LUSSURIOSO That will do well. – Base rogue, thou
    sleepest thy last. – [A*side*] 'Tis policy to have him
    killed in's sleep, for if he waked, he would betray all
    to them.   50

VINDICE But, my lord –

LUSSURIOSO Ha, what say'st?

VINDICE Shall we kill him now he's drunk?

LUSSURIOSO Aye, best of all.

VINDICE Why, then he will ne'er live to be sober.   55

LUSSURIOSO No matter, let him reel to hell.

VINDICE But being so full of liquor, I fear he will put
    out all the fire.

LUSSURIOSO Thou art a mad beast.

VINDICE [*aside*] And leave none to warm your lordship's   60

golls withal, for he that dies drunk falls into hellfire like
a bucket o' water, qush, qush.

USSURIOSO   Come, be ready! Nake your swords, think
of your wrongs. This slave has injured you.

VINDICE   Troth, so he has! – [*aside*] and he has paid well   65
for 't.

USSURIOSO   Meet with him now.

VINDICE   You'll bear us out, my lord?

USSURIOSO   Puh, am I a lord for nothing, think you?
Quickly now.   70

VINDICE   Sa, sa, sa!

　　　[*Vindice and Hippolito stab the corpse, which falls
　　　forward*]
　　　　　　　　　Thump, there he lies.

USSURIOSO   Nimbly done.
　　　[*Approaches the corpse*]
　　　　　　　　　　　Ha! O, villains, murderers,
'Tis the old duke my father!

VINDICE   That's a jest.

USSURIOSO   What, stiff and cold already?
O pardon me to call you from your names;   75
'Tis none of your deed. That villain Piato,
Whom you thought now to kill, has murdered him
And left him thus disguised.

HIPPOLITO   And not unlikely.

VINDICE   O rascal! Was he not ashamed
To put the duke into a greasy doublet?   80

USSURIOSO   He has been cold and stiff, who knows
how long?

VINDICE [*aside*]   Marry, that do I.

USSURIOSO   No words, I pray, of anything intended.

VINDICE   O, my lord.

HIPPOLITO   I would fain have your lordship think that   85
we have small reason to prate.

LUSSURIOSO   Faith, thou say'st true. I'll forthwith send
    to court
    For all the nobles, bastard, duchess, all,
    How here by miracle we found him dead,
    And in his raiment that foul villain fled.   9
VINDICE   That will be the best way, my lord, to clear us
    all; let's cast about to be clear.
LUSSURIOSO   Ho, Nencio, Sordido, and the rest!
        Enter [Nencio, Sordido, and] all [his servants]
FIRST SERVANT   My lord.
SECOND SERVANT   My lord.   9
LUSSURIOSO   Be witnesses of a strange spectacle.
    Choosing for private conference that sad room,
    We found the duke my father gealed in blood.
FIRST SERVANT   My lord the duke! – Run, hie thee, Nencio,
    Startle the court by signifying so much.   10
        [Exit Nencio]
VINDICE *[aside]*   Thus much by wit a deep revenger can:
    When murder's known, to be the clearest man.
    We're furthest off, and with as bold an eye
    Survey his body as the standers-by.
LUSSURIOSO   My royal father, too basely let blood   10
    By a malevolent slave.
HIPPOLITO *[aside to Vindice]*   Hark,
    He calls thee slave again.
VINDICE *[aside to Hippolito]*   H'as lost; he may.
LUSSURIOSO   O sight!
    Look hither, see, his lips are gnawn with poison.
VINDICE   How, his lips? By th' mass, they be.   11
LUSSURIOSO   O villain! O rogue! O slave! O rascal!
HIPPOLITO *[aside]*   O good deceit; he quits him with
    like terms.
        *[Enter two Nobles, Guards, Gentlemen, Ambitioso
        and Supervacuo]*

FIRST NOBLE   Where?

SECOND NOBLE   Which way?

AMBITIOSO   Over what roof hangs this prodigious comet   115
    In deadly fire?

LUSSURIOSO   Behold, behold, my lords:
    The duke my father's murdered by a vassal
    That owes this habit, and here left disguised.
        [*Enter Duchess and Spurio*]

DUCHESS   My lord and husband!

SECOND NOBLE   Reverend majesty!

FIRST NOBLE   I have seen these clothes often attending
    on him.   120

VINDICE [*aside*]   That nobleman has been i' th' country,
    for he does not lie!

SUPERVACUO [*aside to Ambitioso*]   Learn of our mother;
    let's dissemble too.
    I'm glad he's vanished; so, I hope, are you?

AMBITIOSO [*aside to Supervacuo*]   Aye, you may take my
    word for 't.

SPURIO [*aside*]   Old dad, dead?   125
    I, one of his cast sins, will send the fates
    Most hearty commendations by his own son.
    I'll tug in the new stream till strength be done.

LUSSURIOSO   Where be those two that did affirm to us
    My lord the duke was privately rid forth?   130

FIRST GENTLEMAN   O, pardon us, my lords; he gave
    that charge
    Upon our lives, if he were missed at court,
    To answer so. He rode not anywhere;
    We left him private with that fellow here.

VINDICE [*aside*]   Confirmed.

LUSSURIOSO   O heavens, that false charge was his death.   135
    Impudent beggars! durst you to our face

Maintain such a false answer? Bear him straight
To execution.
FIRST GENTLEMAN   My lord!
LUSSURIOSO   Urge me no more.
In this, the excuse may be called half the murder!
VINDICE [*aside*]   You've sentenced well.
LUSSURIOSO   Away, see it be done.   140
[*Exit First Gentleman, guarded*]
VINDICE [*aside*]   Could you not stick? See what confession
doth!
Who would not lie when men are hanged for truth?
HIPPOLITO [*aside to Vindice*]   Brother, how happy is our
vengeance.
VINDICE   [*aside to Hippolito*]   Why, it hits
Past the apprehension of indifferent wits.
LUSSURIOSO   My lord, let post-horse be sent   145
Into all places to entrap the villain.
VINDICE [*aside*]   Post-horse! ha, ha.
[FIRST] NOBLE   My lord, we're something bold to know
our duty.
Your father's accidentally departed;
The titles that were due to him meet you.   150
LUSSURIOSO   Meet me? I'm not at leisure, my good lord;
I've many griefs to dispatch out o' th' way. –
[*Aside*] Welcome, sweet titles! – Talk to me, my lords,
Of sepulchres and mighty emperors' bones;
That's thought for me.
VINDICE   [*aside*]   So one may see by this   155
How foreign markets go:
Courtiers have feet o' th' nines, and tongues o' th'
twelves;
They flatter dukes, and dukes flatter themselves.
[SECOND] NOBLE   My lord, it is your shine must
comfort us.

LUSSURIOSO   Alas, I shine in tears, like the sun in April.   160
FIRST] NOBLE   Y'are now my lord's grace.
LUSSURIOSO   My lord's grace!
   I perceive you'll have it so.
FIRST] NOBLE   'Tis but your own.
LUSSURIOSO   Then heavens give me grace to be so.
VINDICE [*aside*]   He prays well for himself.
SECOND] NOBLE   [*to the Duchess*]   Madam,
   All sorrows must run their circles into joys.   165
   No doubt but time will make the murderer
   Bring forth himself.
VINDICE   [*aside*]   He were an ass then, i' faith.
FIRST] NOBLE   In the mean season,
   Let us bethink the latest funeral honours
   Due to the duke's cold body – and, withal,   170
   Calling to memory our new happiness,
   Spread in his royal son. Lords, gentlemen,
   Prepare for revels.
VINDICE   [*aside*]   Revels!
SECOND] NOBLE   Time hath several falls;
   Griefs lift up joys, feasts put down funerals.
LUSSURIOSO   Come then, my lords, my favours to you all.   175
   [*Aside*]   The duchess is suspected foully bent;
   I'll begin dukedom with her banishment.
     Exeunt Lussurioso, Nobles, Duchess, [Sordido, and
     Servants]
HIPPOLITO [*aside to Vindice*]   Revels!
VINDICE [*aside to Hippolito*]   Aye, that's the word; we
     are firm yet;
   Strike one strain more, and then we crown our wit.   180
     Exeunt [Vindice and Hippolito]
SPURIO [*aside*]   Well, have [at] the fairest mark!
   So said the duke when he begot me;
   And if I miss his heart or near about,

Then have at any; a bastard scorns to be out.
    [*Exit Spurio*]
SUPERVACUO   Note'st thou that Spurio, brother?   185
AMBITIOSO   Yes, I note him to our shame.
SUPERVACUO   He shall not live, his hair shall not grow
   much longer. In this time of revels, tricks may be set
   afoot. Seest thou yon new moon? It shall outlive the
   new duke by much; this hand shall dispossess him,   190
   then we're mighty.
   A mask is treason's license – that build upon;
   'Tis murder's best face when a vizard's on.
     Exit Supervacuo
AMBITIOSO   Is't so? 'tis very good;
   And do you think to be duke then, kind brother?   195
   I'll see fair play: drop one, and there lies t'other.
     Exit

Act V Scene II

*Enter Vindice and Hippolito, with Piero and other
Lords*

VINDICE   My lords, be all of music;
   Strike old griefs into other countries
   That flow in too much milk and have faint livers,
   Not daring to stab home their discontents.
   Let our hid flames break out, as fire, as lightning,   5
   To blast this villainous dukedom vexed with sin;
   Wind up your souls to their full height again.
PIERO   How?
FIRST LORD   Which way?
THIRD LORD   Any way; our wrongs are such,

We cannot justly be revenged too much.

VINDICE   You shall have all enough. Revels are toward,   10
And those few nobles that have long suppressed you
Are busied to the furnishing of a masque,
And do affect to make a pleasant tale on't;
The masquing suits are fashioning – now comes in
That which must glad us all: we to take pattern   15
Of all those suits, the colour, trimming, fashion,
E'en to an undistinguished hair almost.
Then, ent'ring first, observing the true form,
Within a strain or two we shall find leisure
To steal our swords out handsomely,   20
And when they think their pleasure sweet and good,
In midst of all their joys, they shall sigh blood.

PIERO   Weightily, effectually!

THIRD LORD   Before the t'other masquers come –

VINDICE   We're gone, all done and past.   25

PIERO   But how for the duke's guard?

VINDICE   Let that alone;
By one and one their strengths shall be drunk down.

HIPPOLITO There are five hundred gentlemen in the
    action,
That will apply themselves, and not stand idle.

PIERO   O, let us hug your bosoms!

VINDICE   Come, my lords,   30
Prepare for deeds; let other times have words.
    Exeunt

Act V Scene III

*In a dumb show, the possessing of Lussurioso, with
[three] Nobles; then sounding music. A furnished*

table is brought forth; then enters [again] Lussurioso
and his Nobles to the banquet. A blazing star
appeareth

[FIRST] NOBLE   Many harmonious hours and choicest
    pleasures
  Fill up the royal numbers of your years.

LUSSURIOSO   My lords, we're pleased to thank you –
    though we know
  'Tis but your duty now to wish it so.

[SECOND] NOBLE   That shine makes us all happy.

THIRD NOBLE   [*aside*]   His grace frowns.

SECOND NOBLE [*aside*]   Yet we must say he smiles.

FIRST NOBLE   [*aside*]   I think we must.

LUSSURIOSO   [*aside*] That foul, incontinent duchess we
    have banished;
  The bastard shall not live. After these revels,
  I'll begin strange ones; he and the stepsons
  Shall pay their lives for the first subsidies.
  We must not frown so soon, else 't had been now.

FIRST NOBLE   My gracious lord, please you prepare for
    pleasure;
  The masque is not far off.

LUSSURIOSO   We are for pleasure.
  [*To the star*] Beshrew thee! what art thou, mad'st me
    start?
  Thou hast committed treason. [*To the Nobles*] A
    blazing star!

FIRST NOBLE   A blazing star? O where, my lord?

LUSSURIOSO   Spy out.

SECOND NOBLE   See, see, my lords, a wondrous
    dreadful one!

LUSSURIOSO   I am not pleased at that ill-knotted fire,
  That bushing, flaring star. Am not I duke?
  It should not quake me now; had it appeared

Before it, I might then have justly feared.
But yet they say, whom art and learning weds,
When stars wear locks they threaten great men's heads.
Is it so? You are read, my lords.
FIRST NOBLE   May it please your grace,
   It shows great anger.
LUSSURIOSO   That does not please our grace.   25
SECOND NOBLE   Yet here's the comfort, my lord: many
      times,
   When it seems most, it threatens farthest off.
LUSSURIOSO   Faith, and I think so too.
FIRST NOBLE   Beside, my lord,
   You're gracefully established with the loves
   Of all your subjects; and for natural death,   30
   I hope it will be threescore years a-coming.
LUSSURIOSO   True. No more but threescore years?
FIRST NOBLE   Fourscore, I hope, my lord.
SECOND NOBLE   And fivescore, I.
THIRD NOBLE   But 'tis my hope, my lord, you shall ne'er die.
LUSSURIOSO   Give me thy hand, these others I rebuke;   35
   He that hopes so is fittest for a duke.
   Thou shalt sit next me. Take your places, lords;
   We're ready now for sports; let 'em set on.
   [*To the star*] You thing, we shall forget you quite anon!
THIRD NOBLE   I hear 'em coming, my lord.
      Enter the masque of revengers: Vindice, Hippolito, and
      two lords more
LUSSURIOSO   Ah, 'tis well. –   40
   [*Aside*] Brothers, and bastard, you dance next in hell.
      The revengers dance; at the end, steal out their
      swords, and these four kill the four at the table, in
      their chairs. It thunders
VINDICE   Mark, thunder!
   Dost know thy cue, thou big-voiced crier?

Dukes' groans are thunder's watchwords.
HIPPOLITO   So, my lords, you have enough.   45
VINDICE   Come, let's away, no ling'ring.
HIPPOLITO   Follow! Go!
    Exeunt [revengers except Vindice]
VINDICE   No power is angry when the lustful die;
    When thunder claps, heaven likes the tragedy.
    Exit Vindice
LUSSURIOSO   O, O.
    *Enter the other masque of intended murderers:
    Ambitioso, Supervacuo, Spurio, and a Fourth Man,
    coming in dancing. Lussurioso recovers a little in
    voice, and groans – calls 'A guard, treason.' At
    which they all start out of their measure, and turning
    towards the table, they find them all to be murdered*
SPURIO   Whose groan was that?
LUSSURIOSO   Treason, a guard.   50
AMBITIOSO   How now? All murdered!
SUPERVACUO   Murdered!
FOURTH MAN   And those his nobles!
AMBITIOSO   Here's a labour saved;
    I thought to have sped him. 'Sblood, how came this?
[SUPERVACUO] Then I proclaim myself; now I am duke.
AMBITIOSO   Thou duke! brother, thou liest.
    [*Stabs Supervacuo*]
SPURIO   Slave, so dost thou!   55
    [*Stabs Ambitioso*]
FOURTH MAN   Base villain, hast thou slain my lord and
    master?
    [*Stabs Spurio.*] *Enter Vindice, Hippolito, and the two
    Lords*
VINDICE   Pistols! treason! murder! help! Guard my lord
    The duke!
    [*Enter Antonio and Guards*]

HIPPOLITO   Lay hold upon this traitor.
        [*They seize the Fourth Man*]
LUSSURIOSO   O.
VINDICE   Alas, the duke is murdered.
HIPPOLITO   And the nobles.
VINDICE   Surgeons, surgeons! [*Aside*] Heart! does he
        breathe so long?   60
ANTONIO   A piteous tragedy! able to wake
    An old man's eyes bloodshot.
LUSSURIOSO   O.
VINDICE   Look to my lord the duke! [*Aside*] A
        vengeance throttle him.
    [*To Fourth Man*] Confess, thou murd'rous and
        unhallowed man,
    Didst thou kill all these?
FOURTH MAN   None but the bastard, I.   65
VINDICE   How came the duke slain, then?
FOURTH MAN   We found him so.
LUSSURIOSO   O villain.
VINDICE   Hark.
LUSSURIOSO   Those in the masque did murder us.
VINDICE   Law you now, sir.
    O marble impudence! will you confess now?
FOURTH MAN   'Slud, 'tis all false!
ANTONIO   Away with that foul monster,   70
    Dipped in a prince's blood.
FOURTH MAN   Heart, 'tis a lie!
ANTONIO   Let him have bitter execution.
        [*Exit Fourth Man, guarded*]
VINDICE [*aside*] New marrow! No, I cannot be expressed. –
    How fares my lord the duke?
LUSSURIOSO   Farewell to all;
    He that climbs highest has the greatest fall.   75

My tongue is out of office.
VINDICE   Air, gentlemen, air!
    [*The others step back. Vindice whispers to Lussurioso*]
  Now thou'lt not prate on't, 'twas Vindice murdered
    thee –
LUSSURIOSO   O.
VINDICE [*whispers*]   Murdered thy father –
LUSSURIOSO   O.
VINDICE   [*whispers*]   – And I am he.
  Tell nobody.
    [*Lussurioso dies*]
    [*Aloud*]   So, so, the duke's departed.
ANTONIO   It was a deadly hand that wounded him;   8o
  The rest, ambitious who should rule and sway
  After his death, were so made all away.
VINDICE   My lord was unlikely.
HIPPOLITO   [*to Antonio*]   Now the hope
  Of Italy lies in your reverend years.
VINDICE   Your hair will make the silver age again,   8o
  When there was fewer but more honest men.
ANTONIO   The burden's weighty and will press age down.
  May I so rule that heaven may keep the crown.
VINDICE   The rape of your good lady has been quited
  With death on death.
ANTONIO   Just is the law above.   9o
  But of all things it puts me most to wonder
  How the old duke came murdered.
VINDICE   O, my lord.
ANTONIO   It was the strangeliest carried; I not heard of
    the like.
HIPPOLITO   'Twas all done for the best, my lord.
VINDICE   All for your grace's good. We may be bold   9o
  To speak it now. 'Twas somewhat witty carried,
  Though we say it; 'twas we two murdered him.

ANTONIO   You two?

VINDICE   None else, i' faith, my lord; nay, 'twas well
    managed.

ANTONIO   Lay hands upon those villains.
    [*Guards seize them*]

VINDICE   How! on us?   100

ANTONIO   Bear 'em to speedy execution.

VINDICE   Heart! was't not for your good, my lord?

ANTONIO   My good? Away with 'em. Such an old man
    as he!
  You that would murder him would murder me.

VINDICE   Is't come about?

HIPPOLITO   'Sfoot, brother, you begun.   105

VINDICE   May not we set as well as the duke's son?
  Thou hast no conscience: are we not revenged?
  Is there one enemy left alive amongst those?
  'Tis time to die, when we are ourselves our foes.
  When murd'rers shut deeds close, this curse does seal
    'em: 110
  If none disclose 'em, they themselves reveal 'em.
  This murder might have slept in tongueless brass,
  But for ourselves, and the world died an ass.
  Now I remember too, here was Piato
  Brought forth a knavish sentence once: 115
  No doubt, said he, but time
  Will make the murderer bring forth himself.
  'Tis well he died; he was a witch. –
  And now, my lord, since we are in forever:
  This work was ours, which else might have been
    slipped;   120
  And if we list, we could have nobles clipped
  And go for less than beggars; but we hate
  To bleed so cowardly. We have enough,
  I' faith, we're well: our mother turned, our sister true,

We die after a nest of dukes – adieu.   12

> *Exeunt* [*Vindice and Hippolito, guarded*]

ANTONIO   How subtly was that murder closed! Bear up
Those tragic bodies; 'tis a heavy season.
Pray heaven their blood may wash away all treason.
> [*Exeunt*]

Notes

sd = stage direction

The Persons of the Play

Many of the characters bear allegorical names like those used in morality plays. Most are to be found in John Florio's dictionary *A Worlde of Wordes* (1598).

Lussurioso   lecherous.
Spurio   false, illegitimate.
Ambitioso   ambitious.
Supervacuo   superfluous, vain or empty.
Vindice   revenger.
Piato   hidden.
Dondolo   fool.
Gratiana   grace.
Castiza   chastity.

Act I Scene I

The play opens with a morality-style procession of Vices introduced by Vindice (see Interpretations page 154). The use of *torchlight* establishes the dominant motif of the link between night-time, darkness and sin. The second half of this scene becomes private; in a family discussion, the wrongs inflicted by the corrupt Duke are revealed. The prospect of the first revenge (for Gloriana) is established.

4 **do**   copulate.
5–6 **O, that marrowless... damned desires**   Vindice wonders at the effect of *age* on the Duke; his body is filled with evil *desires*.
7 **infernal fires**   both the eternal flames of hell and the sensation of burning linked to venereal disease.

8 **dry**   sterile and withered.

9 **luxur**   lecher.

11 **like a son and heir**   The sons of rich noblemen, expecting to inherit large amounts of money, spent vast sums to promote themselves at court and lived for pleasure; James I himself also spent lavishly (see Interpretations page 207–8).

13 **fret**   This is a pun meaning both 'anger' and the ridge that controls the strings of a musical instrument.

14 **Thou sallow picture**   Vindice addresses the pale skull of Gloriana. The striking image of the protagonist addressing a skull recalls the gravedigger's scene in Shakespeare's *Hamlet* (V.i). See Interpretations pages 197–201.

15 **study**   serious thought, as well as the place where he might go to think and read.

19 **two heaven-pointed diamonds**   i.e. Gloriana's eyes. Vindice compares the beauty of diamonds, symbols of eternity, to that of his short-lived fiancée. Compare I.iii.9.

20 **unsightly**   This is a pun on 'unseeing' and 'ugly'.

22 **bought complexion**   face made up with expensive cosmetics.

25 **after**   at.

26 **usurer**   one who lends money at high rates of interest.

27 **patrimony**   inheritance.

28 **told**   counted and collected.

29 **cold**   unsuccessful.

31 **appareled**   clothed.

34 **palsy**   condition (associated with age) causing an uncontrollable trembling.

34–6 **old men… limited performances**   Vindice comments that the lust of old men, like the anger of young men, is soon spent.

36 **Outbid**   inadequate, overcome by others who are stronger.

37 **'ware**   beware.

38 This is the first of the many *sententiae* or moral sayings in the play.

39 **quit-rent**   fee paid by a *tenant* (line 40) for services. Revenge is the fee due for murder.

42 **determined**   judged.

42–3 **who e'er knew… unpaid**   whoever found murder going unpunished.

44 **Sh'as kept touch**   she (*Revenge*) has kept her part of the bargain.
Be merry   Vindice addresses the skull directly.

45–7 **fat folks… bare as this**   The fattest, fleshiest person will one day be reduced to the *bare*ness of the skull; *three-piled* is the finest, thickest velvet.

48 **great**   This is a pun meaning both important or powerful, and large.
clay   flesh (which is made of earth). Vindice is introducing the motif of the deceptiveness of appearances, as the proudest human being is ultimately *clay*.

49 **little**   of low rank.

50 **vizard**   mask or face.

51 **how go things**   This is interpreted by Hippolito (see the next line) as a pun meaning both 'how are matters' and 'how do the (less-than-human) courtiers go about'.

52 **braver**   more showy.

55 **Opportunity**   Vindice introduces the problem of overcoming delays in his revenge, one of the conventions of revenge drama.

56 **happy**   in luck.

57 **scabbard**   sheath for a dagger or sword.

63 **hold by th'duchess' skirt**   i.e. hold onto my favour with the Duchess. Is there a suggestion that Hippolito's favour is sexual? Line 64 could be interpreted as sexual innuendo.

69 **By policy**   cunningly, indirectly.
open and unhusk me   interrogate me, sound me out.

71–2 **keep… houses**   keep my opinions to myself.

73 **An idle satisfaction**   i.e. a little harmless information.

76 **strange-digested**   of a strange, unsettled temperament.

79 **blood**   man of high spirits. Compare this to the other 'blood' imagery in the play.

81 **base-coined**   lowly born. This metaphor linking having children with coining money forms part of the imagery of usury (compare II.ii.144.)
pander   go-between (in sexual affairs).

82 **reach**   understand.

83 **concubines**   women who lived with a man without being legally married; mistresses.

85–9 His lust would refuse no woman, however ugly or diseased.

89 **unsound**   unhealthy, especially suffering from syphilis.

93 **put on**   disguise myself as. The imagery of disguise and the wearing of masks emerges.

94 **right** true. Vindice is speaking ironically.

97 **prefer** recommend for employment or promotion.

101 **French mole** Just as the mole's digging undermines a garden, so the 'French disease' syphilis causes hair loss.

102 **habit** costume.

103 **coin** pretend, with a pun on 'make counterfeit money'.

106 **swallow** believe (false things).

108 **Carlo** This is perhaps an error; or Hippolito has changed his name for the court; or it could be his mother's pet-name for him.

110 **played** committed.

113 **If** even if.

 hopes i.e. for the next generation of rulers.

115 **The law's a woman** Traditionally, justice is presented as female, as it is in the statue at the Old Bailey courts in London.

119–21 There is a clear echo of *Hamlet* here; Shakespeare's prince likewise describes at the beginning of the play the effect his grief for the death of his father has had upon him (*Hamlet*, I.ii.129–37).

123 Gratiana regrets that her husband's *estate* (wealth, position) was not equal to the worth of his *mind*.

124 **deject** humiliate.

125–6 **smothered in… mount** repressed his ability and ambition when it would show itself.

129 **midnight secretary** private confidant at all hours.

134 **turn into another** put on my disguise.

Act I Scene II

The scene opens with Junior, guarded by Officers, standing trial for the rape of Antonio's wife. It is a cameo of the corrupt justice of the Duke's court. In the last part of the scene, further revenges are planned: by the Duchess on the Duke, and by Spurio on both the Duke and Lussurioso. How do these differ from Vindice's revenge?

4 **forehead** This is one of many references to the *forehead*; see line 33, and I.iii.8. The forehead was associated with a sense of *shame* (line 10) and modesty. See also Note to line 107 below.

10 **closest**   most secret.

11 **silver**   grey-haired, i.e. mature.

13 **insculption**   inscription carved into stone.

14 **bowelled**   disembowelled and embalmed.

15 **cered**   sealed in waxed fabric (the *cerecloths* in the next line).

20 **fact**   deed.

24 **son-in-law**   stepson.

29 **Gilt**   gilded (covered with gold). Is there also a pun on 'guilt'?

36 **corse**   corpse.

37 **fruitless**   without success; also, without her child.

38–9 **Are my… without respect**   am I of such ignoble origins that kneeling to you gains no respect.

41 **doom**   judgement.

42 **attempt**   assault.

46 **general-honest**   wholly virtuous.

57–8 **if our tongues… the fact**   if we did not punish the crime adequately.

63 **die**   This is a pun on the two meanings of 'die' as physical death and sexual climax.

65 **'sessed**   assessed, judged.

75 **performance**   i.e. sexual performance.

79 **too much right**   too strict a reading of the law.

82 **dad**   This over-familiar term is disrespectful in the context; see Interpretations pages 160 and 193–4.

85 **makes for**   helps, favours.

95 **easy**   compliant, willing.

103 **durance**   imprisonment.

107 **kill him in his forehead**   i.e. take revenge by making him a cuckold. The cuckold (husband of an unfaithful wife) was said to have horns on his forehead.

111 **wealthy**   i.e. bestowing wealth.

117 **My duty on your hand**   I kiss your hand as a token of my respect.

123 **hatted dame**   lower-class woman. Women at court did not wear hats.

125 **Idle**   foolish.

137 **ride a horse well**   Because of the verb *ride*, this suggests skills in sexual matters also.

   marry   an oath ('by St Mary').

140 **'light**   alight (from his horse).

125

141 **penthouse** awning above shop fronts.

142 **check** knock against.
barbers' basins These metal dishes were hung outside shop fronts to advertise services.

143 The Duchess teases Spurio with a sexual pun.

148 **bid fair for't** tried for it, seemed near achieving it.

149–50 **a right diamond ... dukedom's ring** This continues the jewellery imagery of the play; compare I.i.19–20.

152 **collet** setting on a ring for a stone.

161 **seventh commandment** In the Bible, the seventh of God's ten commandments forbids adultery.

164 **hot-backed** lustful.

165 **blood** temper. This is another example of the blood imagery of the play.

170 **venial** pardonable.

173 **Earnest** pledge, or foretaste.

176 **woman's heraldry** i.e. the cuckold's horns on a betrayed husband's forehead (see Note to line 107). See also line 201, and II.ii.165.

180 **stirring** stimulating.

181 **healths** toasts (drinks in honour of something or someone).

184 **thick** i.e. with speech affected by drunkenness.

185 **fall again** i.e. to lie down with a man.

194 **confusion** ruin.

196 **the duke's only son** Lussurioso.

197 **beholding to report** publicly respected.

200 **loose my days upon him** spend my time on (plotting against) him.

Act I Scene III

The disguised Vindice accepts Lussurioso's commission as a way of working towards his revenge on the Duke; he is then forced to become involved in Lussurioso's attempted seduction of his own sister.

1 **far enough from myself** sufficiently well disguised.

3 **wist** knew.

12 **scholar** These were traditionally regarded as lacking in worldly wisdom.

13 **maid in the old time** virgin from times gone by.

17 **you reach out o' th' verge** you're going too far.

18 **'Sfoot** 'God's foot', an oath.

23 **rare** excellent.

24–5 **if Time/ Had so much hair** The figure of *Time* was traditionally presented as bald.

28 **words are but great men's blanks** words are cheap for powerful men. *Blanks* are documents with spaces left to be filled, or metal not yet stamped with a hallmark.

34 **muskcat** lover, or prostitute. Some directors pick up on descriptions such as this to suggest that Lussurioso is bisexual.

36 **Gather** encourage, incite.

37 **ague** fever.

39 **Forget myself** forget my royal status.

40 **remember me** remember who I am.

41 **conster** consider or construe.

43 **bone-setter** person who re-sets broken or dislocated bones.

45 **sets bones together** i.e. brings bodies together, for sex.

47 **trained up to my hand** trained to do exactly what I wish.

48 **scrivener** secretary, clerk.

51 **patrimonies washed a-pieces** i.e. estates broken up to provide money for drunken revelry; see Interpretations page 207.

51–2 **fruit fields turned into bastards** i.e. family land sold in defiance of the usual practice of inheritance.

54 **gravel** serve as sand for. Sand would be strewn on parchment documents to dry the ink.

57 **Dutch** The Dutch and Germans were stereotyped as heavy drinkers, so this term implies 'excessive' or 'drunken'.

77 **near employment** private task.

80 **disease o' th' mother** hysteria, but here a pun on talking too much (like a woman).

81 **close** closed up, reserved.

85 **in me** in my confidence.

86 **enter** possess, with a pun on sexual penetration.

Indian devil   Gold and silver came from the Indies.

93 **waxed lines**   sealed letters.

neatest   most intense.

98 **phoenix**   paragon; a mythical bird famed for its excellence.

repugnant   resistant.

101 **blood**   family.

102 **mean**   lowly, inferior.

good enough to be bad withal   i.e. good enough to provoke my desires, and poor enough to make her a suitable target.

104 **friend**   mistress.

110 **luxurious**   lecherous, lustful.

112 **cozen**   cheat.

115 **bring it into expense**   make her spend it.

118 **gi'en 't the tang**   caught the flavour of it, got it right.

120 **move it**   promote it, make it work.

125 **late**   recent.

129 **put a man in**   suggest what a man could say. Castiza's *bodkin* (blunt thick needle, or hairpin) will presumably suggest sexual puns to Vindice.

138 **simple age**   youth and gullibility.

141 **wind up**   recruit, encourage.

155 **in league with**   associated with.

159 **furnish thee**   provide what you need.

164 Before long, you can expect to be in a higher position in life.

172 **disheir**   disinherit him as heir to the dukedom (i.e. by killing him).

173 **down**   under control.

174 **meanest policy**   most despicable of plans.

175 **both**   i.e. his mother and sister.

178 **o'erwrought**   won over.

179 **thought travelled**   believed to be away on a journey.

179–80 **apply myself/ Unto the selfsame form**   try to do the same task.

182 **touch**   test.

for good   in the name of goodness.

183 **blood**   temperament, virtue.

Act I Scene IV

In a complete change of mood, Antonio laments his wife's death and Hippolito pledges to revenge her. For the second time in the play, a dead female victim is presented to the audience. What is the effect of this?

1 sd   Presumably a curtain is drawn back to reveal the body of Antonio's wife in its symbolic pose, perhaps in a curtained discovery space (see Interpretations page 182).

5   **strikes man out of me**   takes away my manly strength.

11   **pledge**   drink to.

14   **confection**   both her means of preserving her goodness, and her design in choosing to die in this pose.

15   **tucked up**   folded over.

17   'It is better to die virtuous than live dishonoured.' This is an echo of the Roman historian Livy's account of the actions of Lucretia, the wife of a Roman general who similarly committed suicide after being raped (see Interpretations page 202).

23   'Lesser cares can speak, greater cares are silent.' This echoes Seneca, a Roman writer.

31   **moth**   Junior is a *moth* in that he eats away her *honour* as a moth eats fabric.

32   **Filled up a room**   took a place.

33   **wearing**   clothing, i.e. his honour and his wife (picking up the fabric image).

40   **but for relation**   except for the need to tell you.

41   **vizard**   mask.

42   **harried**   violated.

43   **damnation of both kinds**   sinning themselves and corrupting others; or, the sins of both men and women.

46   **dowry**   legacy.

48   **of rare fire compact**   made of the rarest elements.

49   **empress**   This is a pun suggesting nobility and also the impression made when valuable metal is stamped.

61   **Judgement speak all in gold**   justice is perverted by wealth and power.

64   **swear**   This is an ironic echo of Lussurioso's attempt to have Vindice swear to carry out his bidding in I.iii.160.

Act II Scene I

The setting becomes domestic and also has echoes of scenes from a morality play, as the Vice figure, Vindice, unwillingly tempts his mother and sister.

1 **hardly** severely.
  beset besieged, at risk.
2 **constant** steadfast.
3 **child's-part** inheritance.
19 **dirty way** muddy track. Castiza is telling Dondolo to speak more directly, and also without sexual innuendo.
27 **affects** loves.
36 **attorney** (legal) representative.
43 **drawn-work cuff** This is a pun on the embroidered cuff of a sleeve and the cuff or blow that has left a mark on Vindice's cheek.
45 **take the wall** take the side next to the wall, and therefore take precedence.
46 **I'm above my tongue** I'm happier than I can say.
54 **siren** mythical woman whose beautiful singing lured sailors to their deaths.
57 **next** i.e. next in line to the throne.
62 **gapes for him every tide** looks likely to become open to him any time now.
65 **save** except for.
68 **wink** close my eyes.
  Marry an oath ('by St Mary').
71 **wheel** wheel of fortune.
73 **white** i.e. white-haired with age, and also covered in *mould*.
79 **'lack the day** alas.
80 **vex the number** i.e. make the problem worse by multiplying the number.
86 **angels** This is a pun on angels of heaven and gold coins called angels.
91 **dejected** made lowly.
95–100 Vindice itemizes the daughter's physical assets as if valuing an estate where the different items will bring income to the mother.

97 **maintenance** income.

99 **ride** This is a sexual pun; see I.ii.137 and Note.

101 **pains** trouble. This suggests both the *pains* of childbirth and the effort of bringing up a child carefully.

102 **requite** repay.
but some only in part.

103 **bring you home** make you secure and rich.

108 **bate** weaken.

110 **turns edge** becomes dull or blunt.

124 **the mother** maternal feeling, but also a pun on hysteria; see I.iii.80.

126 **blush** a sign of modesty or of guilt. See IV.iv.44.

127 **invisible finger** This is probably a reference to biblical stories of Belshazzar's corrupt feasting, drinking and love of wealth (Daniel 5), where an *invisible finger* wrote on a wall in blood about his sins. Belshazzar was murdered. This is one of the supernatural references found throughout the play.

138 **dam** (animal) mother.

150 **betters** social superiors.

155 **come by your selves** access your own treasure.

165 **owe your cheek my hand** ought to slap your face.

171 **rich** valuable because of scarcity.

183 **keep less charge** both maintain less expense and worry less about virtue.

188 **forehead** See Note to I.ii.4.

192 **'Slid** an oath.

197 **stirring meats** See I.ii.180 and Note.

199 **quicken** come to life, enliven, and also make pregnant. The *meats* are equated with the people who eat them.

201 **Bareheaded** Men did not wear hats at court.

202 **horns** These were used as hat racks, but the cuckold's horns are also suggested; see Note to I.ii.107.

212 **useless** i.e. sexually useless.

214 **a hundred acres on their backs** i.e. their clothes cost as much as a hundred acres of land (or those acres have been sold to buy the clothes).

215 **green foreparts** This is a pun on the parks in front of country houses and the decorated bodices of women's dress.

218 The *farmers' sons* have exchanged their lives of honest manual work for the life of *gentlemen* at court.
220 **mete by the rod**   measured by the rod (a traditional unit of measurement).
221 **yard**   While farmers measure land by the rod, tailors measure fabric by the yard. The image is of estates being sold in order to finance expensive clothes.
222 **foretops**   front locks of hair arranged decoratively.
223 **head-tires**   head-dresses.
231 **brook it**   bear its loss.
239 **make the mother a disease**   See Note to line 124.
242 **crystal plaudities**   clear, ringing applause.
249 **base-titled creatures that look downward**   beasts, animals.

Act II Scene II

In their second encounter, Vindice has to tell Lussurioso about his failure to corrupt Castiza, and his success in persuading Gratiana to help. He later needs to use his ingenuity to distract Lussurioso from pursuing Castiza in person, by telling him news about a rumoured meeting between the Duchess and Spurio. But Spurio has his own designs on Lussurioso's life.

7 **preferred**   recommended.
19 **toward**   in prospect.
24 **bate in**   lose some.
25 **made indifferent-honest naught**   brought a person of average virtue to ruin.
27 **white**   silver.
28–9 **Many a maid... easier working**   it has been easier to convert many a young woman to the worship of *Mahomet*.
31 **flat**   lay flat.
32 **close**   secure, invulnerable.
36 **be forsworn**   tell a lie.
38 **liv'st not**   shall not live.
43 **did me I**   did I do.
56 **blow fire on her cheeks**   i.e. make her blush.

67 **ravel** unravel.

69–70 **I'll make 'em freemen** I'll give them (*my desires*) freedom.

72 **leg** bow by bending one knee.

78 **drab** mistress, prostitute.

80–81 **have all the fees behind the arras** Vindice could hide in the space between the wall-hanging and the wall and collect a tax on illicit love-making.

81 **farthingales** hooped petticoats.

82 **fall plump** drop abruptly.

83 **rushes** These were strewn on the floors of houses to absorb dirt and smells. They would be regularly swept up and replaced.

84 **apprehensive** witty.

91 **o' th' wrong side** i.e. by stabbing him in the back.

97–8 **O, lessen not… honour her** This is a reference to Exodus 20:12, the commandment to 'Honour thy father and thy mother: that thy days may be long'.

99 **turned my sister into use** i.e. she has become a commodity with a financial value.

103 **beneficial perjury** lie told for an honourable purpose.

110 **pen** pun on 'penis'.

116 **Unbraced** not fully dressed.

133 **additions** honours awarded to add to a coat of arms.

134 **funeral herald's fees** probably both hanging black silk panels used to signify mourning, and heraldry showing the deceased's noble lineage. Heralds were paid *fees* for both.

137 **full sea** high tide.

138 **juggling** deception.

139 **toll-book** document used to list horses for sale at a fair. Its use here compares promiscuous women to animals.

141 **by water** by a side or back entrance that opens onto a river (suggesting the River Thames).

142 **leather hinges** These would make no noise.

143 **proclamation** public exposure.

144 **A-coining** being coined. This term links illicit sex with counterfeit money.

145 **careful sisters spin** This pun links the three Fates who *spin* the *thread* of human destiny to women who use their bodies for profit, as a merchant sells silk.

160 **start** startle.

166 **horn royal**   a royal cuckold, i.e. the Duke.
167 **fruit of two beds**   consequences of adultery.
172 **control**   prevent.
175 He may become violent and spoil his own plans.

Act II Scene III

In an intimate scene set in the Duchess's bedroom, there are opportunities for humour in the Duke's terrified response. The scene might be played with lit torches, and perhaps a curtained bed brought onstage through the central rear entrance. Again, the Duke is seen to change his mind about the administration of justice. What effects are created as events appear to spin out of control here?

  2 **twisted**   physically entwined. The term also suggests perversion.
  5 **spleen**   anger.
11 **penitential heaves**   sighs or sobs of repentance.
12 **unclear**   i.e. with my sins unforgiven.
19 **myself**   i.e. duke.
25 **file**   defile.
33 **eased our swords**   saved our swords the trouble.
43 **out o' th' socket**   out of sequence, dislocated. The light from many torches makes night seem day; possibly the sun is compared to a torch in its wall-socket. See also I.iv.27.
45 The guards are holding Lussurioso by the arms.
59 **Puritan**   hypocritical.
76 **deadly pointed**   like a deadly weapon.
77 **sound**   secure.
78 **Without corrupted favor**   without letting favouritism corrupt his judgement.
81 **Honey**   i.e. sweet words.
90 **moon**   bout of lunacy.
92 **beside your spleen**   without expressing your anger.

98 **signet**   signet-ring or seal, a sign of the Duke's authority.

104 **scarlet hid in lawn**   *Lawn* is very fine linen; it would not cover *scarlet* fabric from view. The image refers to attempts to conceal sin (*scarlet*) with a thin layer of pretence (*lawn*).

117 **mean**   lowly.

128–9 I have poisoned many women who refused me, desiring all (women). *Poison* also carries the sense of moral corruption.

130 **hot**   lustful.

131 **green**   fresh and young.

Act III Scene I

All of Act III except for the central III.v is concerned with the abuse of justice caused by greed and ambition. The malice and folly of Supervacuo and Ambitioso are evident in this scene, as they plan to get rid of Lussurioso.

2 **him**   Lussurioso.

7 **skin of**   cover for.

8 **set by**   pass by, ignore.

14 **puffed out**   blown out (like a candle flame), killed.

16 **packed**   sent packing, got rid of.

17 **wind**   manoeuvre.

24 **set an edge upon the executioner**   This pun means both sharpen the axe used for the execution, and make the executioner hurry.

25 **Meet**   just so.

27 **thou**   i.e. Lussurioso.

Act III Scene II

In this very short scene, Middleton creates dramatic irony in preparation for the scenes that follow.

3 **But** only.
5 **myself** i.e. duke.

Act III Scene III

Ambitioso and Supervacuo's inept attempts to corrupt justice reach a climax. How do the audience know that a misunderstanding is taking place in this scene?

13 **hies** hastens on.
14 **that is** whoever is.
16 **sound** properly or thoroughly carried out.
22 **black** sinful.
24 **be** be in power.
30 **block** This is a pun on the execution block and the block on which hats are shaped; perhaps there is an allusion to Lussurioso's vanity.

Act III Scene IV

The irony continues, as first Junior complains about the lack of help from his brothers, then he is led to execution on their supposed orders.

15–16 **trick... long a-playing** There is a sequence of card-playing imagery here, which suggests that life rests on chance; see line 72 below.
18 **Hang... quarter merry** Traitors suffered the punishment of being hanged, then disembowelled while still alive, and then their bodies were cut up.
20 **lie in** Women would *lie in* for a period of rest and privacy after childbirth. See III.i.18 for another possible example linking this idea to Junior's imprisonment for rape.

40 **sitting**   session of the law courts.
60–61 **worse than. . . salt water**   Ordinary citizens found sea
voyages frightening; they would also have feared being press-
ganged into the navy. Junior is comparing seawater with the *salt
water* of *tears*.
68 **duns**   complicated interpretation.
72 **four cards**   The winning hand in a game of primero was *four
cards* of the same suit.
75 **headsman**   executioner.
78 **cozens**   tricks, deprives.
83 **bleed then. . . of sign**   Junior is punning on the idea of being
bled (as a medical treatment) without regard to the appropriate
astrological *sign* (surgeons usually consulted these), and dying
without special distinction.

Act III Scene V

This powerful and shocking scene forms the centrepiece of the
play. Vindice is finally presented with the opportunity for
revenge that he has craved, and after meditation on the skull of
Gloriana (see Interpretations pages 194 and 197–201), Middleton
presents onstage the brutal torture and death of the Duke. The
liaison between the Duchess and Spurio enacts those very sins of
which the Duke is guilty, in a morality tableau. Vindice also vows
to undertake the second, public aspect of his revenge.

4 **silver ceiling**   starry sky, or richly decorated ceiling in the
palace; and also the 'heavens' or canopy over the stage, which
was painted with suns, moons and stars.
5 **partake**   share, participate.
14 **angle**   corner.
guilty   i.e. has seen guilty acts.
19 **night at noon**   This image of natural and social disorder
seems threatening.
22 **circle**   the enchanted area within which magicians would raise
devils; also suggests the circular stage.

25 **digested** worked out, planned.

26 **missed** excluded.

37 **stoop** submit (i.e. sexually).

38 **common** Hippolito puns on the meanings 'usual' or 'widespread', and 'promiscuous'.

39 **shadowing** secretive.

41 **bare** bareheaded.

42 sd *tires* costumes, clothes.

44 **Secret** Here and in the following lines, Vindice pretends to repeat words that the skull has whispered to him.

51 **all-hid** the call in the game of hide-and-seek.

53 **Age and bare bone** i.e. the Duke (*Age*) and the skull (*bone*).

58 **clasp** clench.

60–61 **wind go whistle./ Spout, rain** Wind and rain are damaging to a woman's make-up.

71 **yellow** the colour of gold and of the *silkworm*'s cocoon.

75 **does yon fellow falsify highways** Travellers could be tricked into taking the wrong road by those who wanted to lure them into unsafe areas in order to rob them. For dramatic effect, Vindice may point to a man in the audience to indicate *yon fellow*.

76 **put his life… judge's lips** risk being sentenced to death by a judge.

77 **refine such a thing** lavish luxurious items on such a lover (to make her *fine*).

84 **Camphor** strong-smelling oil used in make-up and soap.

86 **superfluous outside** i.e. her looks, which are a trivial and temporary matter.

87 **bids** i.e. for her sexual favours.

93 **antic amble** grotesque, drunken movements.

100 **property** stage prop.

101 **it own** its own.

108 **quaintness** originality, ingenuity.

117 **voice** agreement, vote.

119 **absent 'em** send them away.

125–6 **to give… rid forth** to say that I have gone riding privately. The Duke, through his eagerness to commit adultery, plays right into Vindice's hands.

136 **Sh'as** she has.

136–7 **grave look** Vindice intends the Duke to understand 'serious expression', but also means, of course, that she looks like a corpse from a *grave*.

146 **white devil** one who hides evil under a virtuous (*white*) appearance.

148 **hollows** eye-sockets in the skull.

163 **slobbering Dutchman** Dutch men were considered gross and drunken.

177 **rides** This is suggestive of sexual activity, as in I.ii.137.
brow i.e. the place where the cuckold's horns grow.

179 **clips** embraces.

182 **hires** rewards.

184 **quitted** requited, paid back, revenged.

190 **invent** establish, force.

193 **Nail down his tongue** i.e. to stop him talking.

195 **quittance** repay, revenge.

196 **brooking** tolerating.

198 **comets** These were considered omens of disaster; see V.iii.

200 **Whist** hush.

200 sd *kiss* Note the parallel to the Duke kissing the skull; both kisses bring death.

206 **rubs** pushes (an image from the game of bowls).

207 **waxen fire** flame from candles.

211 **hasped** locked (in a sexual embrace).

216 **brook** tolerate. Vindice takes up the other meaning of the word, a stream of water.

218 Vindice comments that it seems fitting for music to be played while a Duke dies; this is another example of his black humour.

219 **though yet unknown** although this is not yet known.

Act III Scene VI

Middleton's stagecraft is evident as he switches the mood from dark tragedy to black humour and farce. Ambitioso and Supervacuo's plans are foiled in the most startling manner, but they of course plot revenge.

 6 **slip** evade.
   in lesser compass of less importance.
 9 **extemporal** immediate.
12 **from you** not in your mind.
19 **next** i.e. next in line.
   honest This is a pun on 'honourable' and 'virtuous'.
22 **he** Lussurioso.
34 **desertless office** thankless task that no one deserves.
39 **fluent** flowing.
55 **Why do you shun me, brothers** What does this indicate
   about the reaction of Ambitioso and Supervacuo at this
   moment?
57 **savour** odour.
80 **prodigious** ominous, threatening.
81 **women** i.e. false, dissembling.
85 **murrain** plague.
90 **Sirrah** This is a disrespectful way to refer to Lussurioso.
   fast securely.

Act IV Scene I

In his role as 'Piato', Vindice is banished after Lussurioso's
disastrous foray into the royal bedroom. But the opportunity
arises for him to be introduced again by Hippolito. The scene
ends with another significant development of the plot as it
becomes known than the Duke is missing from the court.

11 **wittily elected** cleverly chosen. Lussurioso is being sarcastic.
15 **will** intended.
21 **forehead** See Note to I.ii.107.
24 **rased** grazed.
27 **Jars in** interrupts with discordant effect.
35 **iron-age** Lussurioso is punning on the idea of *perpetual*
   imprisonment in iron fetters, and the traditional idea of the
   four ages of the world: gold, silver, brass and iron. The iron age
   was believed to be the last, the worst and the longest.
39 **moved** angered.

49 **repair**   make his way.
50 **blood**   desire, temperament.
58 **succeed**   be the successor.
61 **does himself work to undo him**   does he work to bring about his own undoing.
63 **other slave**   other villain, i.e. Piato.
64–5 **put… into him**   confided in him excessively.
66 **slight**   untrustworthy, unreliable.
68 **speed him**   hurry him on his way, i.e. kill him.
70 **black**   melancholic, depressed.
84 **sudden**   impetuous.
86 **toy**   whim.
87 **light**   frivolous.
88 **oracle**   absolute truth.

Act IV Scene II

In an echo of I.iii, Vindice is hired once again by Lussurioso. What is the effect on the audience of the latter's bare-faced lies? Vindice finds himself hired to undertake yet another of the play's revenges, Lussurioso's vengeance on 'Piato'. Vindice enjoys pointing out the impossibility of his task, but how effectively do he and Hippolito respond to this new complication?

2 **shifts**   tricks, disguises.
5 **quainter fallacy**   cleverer deception.
12 This suggests the idea of killing him using the medieval torture device the 'press', which would crush his *breast*. The instrument Vindice will use to crush him, however, will be the weight of his vengeful *wishes*.
21 **in present**   about what to do now.
25 **least**   least important part of.
  be doubtful   anticipate problems.
31 **gave you out at first in discontent**   initially described you as discontented.

41 sd *makes legs* bows by bending his legs.

42 **How don… god den** How do you do? Good day to you. (Vindice is adopting a polite but unsophisticated style of language used by country folk. Note that from line 48 his speeches are in prose.)

46 **'twould ne'er be stood on't** it would never be tolerated.

50 **buckram** rough fabric that lawyer's bags were made from.

51 *anno quadragesimo secundo* the forty-second year (of the current ruler's reign).

52 *anno sextagesimo tertio* the sixty-third year.

53 **three and twenty years** Lussurioso has made a mistake in his arithmetic, or his Latin.

55 **pullen** poultry.

57 **terms** the four periods of the year when the law-courts sit.

60 **canvassed** brought for investigation.

61 **Barbary** barbarous, uncivilized.

62 **law** legal jargon.

64 **sasarara** English pronunciation of *certiorari*, a writ issued by a higher court when a plaintiff appeals the verdict of a lower court.

71–2 **great chest** strong-box where money and documents are kept.

75 **forfeitures and obligations** losses of goods, lands or bonds; and contracts.

79 **conceit** idea, image.

80 **la** now (common expression in rural speech).

90 **pared** cut. Hippolito recognizes that Vindice has cruelly depicted Lussurioso's own situation, though he himself does not.

99 **cloth-of-gold** expensive fabric woven with gold thread. Lussurioso is probably wearing something similar.

106 **in colours** in appearance (as in a painting).

107 **parlous** dangerous, uncertain.

119 **affect** like, enjoy.

123 **unbrace** reveal.

127 **kept it here** held it back.

135 **wrought with me** pressured or persuaded me.

138 Note the ironic double meanings in both Hippolito's and Vindice's remarks in this shared line, and also in their subsequent comments.

145 **did he me** did he do to me.

154 **for happy** as if good.

168 **wind**   entice, tempt.
172 **y'are put to't**   you're really being tested.
180 **observe**   serve, follow.
185 **in case**   in a condition.
199 **cloven**   split in two. The devil has *cloven* feet.
203 **found it**   thought of a solution.
208 **conveyed**   i.e. his body has not been disposed of.
212 The idea of Vindice disguising and arranging the Duke's corpse recalls his dressing up of Gloriana's skull in III.v, and also echoes the appearance of Antonio's wife's dead body in I.iv.
226 **in grain**   dyed permanently into the fabric (i.e. secure).
227 **hold colour**   i.e. maintain appearances, prove reliable. Vindice is continuing the image of the previous line.

Act IV Scene III

In this short scene, the Duchess's two sons plan yet another revenge, this time upon Spurio. This scene forms an ironic parallel with II.i and especially IV.iv, where Vindice and Hippolito's concern for their mother offers a striking contrast to the attitude of the Duchess's sons towards her.

1 sd *seemeth*   behaves.
  3 **or this or these**   either this or these. The Duchess is presumably referring to the embrace and kisses that she gives to Spurio.
 10 **bent lasciviously**   inclined to be lascivious.
 11 **sleep soft**   live in luxury.

Act IV Scene IV

This scene responds to the events of II.i, where Vindice was so distressed by his mother's weakness. Gratiana's recovery of Christian virtue (the 'grace' implied in her name) holds firm under Castiza's testing.

1 sd The brothers hold onto their mother from either side, just as they held onto the Duke in III.v.

  5 **iron nipples** i.e. the daggers placed at her breast.

  7 **quarled** curdled.

  8 **Cut not your days** do not shorten your life. See Note to II.ii.97–8.

12 **office** duty (as a mother).

14 **powers on high** i.e. God.

17 **of the world's condition** worldly, corrupt.

27 **grace** virtue, grace given by God.

32 **Tried** tested (as *metal* is tested to assess its purity).

39 **I kneel to you** A child was expected always to defer to parents, so Gratiana's gesture of humility before her sons is striking.

40 **give aim to** target.

43 Vindice addresses his dagger, which has drawn his mother's *tears*.

44 **change to red** i.e. rust (the literal version of the *blush* of shame).

45 **it rains** Gratiana's tears are turned into a natural image, which suggests their appropriateness.

47–50 Vindice continues the image of natural fruitfulness.

52 **infectious** infected.

60 **seld** seldom found.

62 **of easy wax** easily moulded or persuaded.

63 **leprously** This is an example of the disease imagery of the play; Gratiana's bad deeds would have marked her like a leper's sores.

64 **forehead** See Note to I.ii.4.

68 **Green-coloured** inexperienced, suffering from the anaemia of a growing girl.

69 **hire** i.e. the payment due to a prostitute.

70 That would have been another torment (like being *boiled* in *lead*).

72 **cloth-o'-silver** expensive fabric woven with silver thread. See I.i.52.

81 **ice** i.e. the ice of chastity.

86 **holy-watered mead** Vindice compares his mother to a meadow sprinkled with the *holy water* of her tears; see lines 45–50.

96 **forehead** expression (of either shame, or boldness; see Note to I.ii.4).

104 **usury** use for profit. This is a central image of the play.

108 **marble**   i.e. hardened, emotionless, so unable to feel shame.
117   There is a pun on *Sons*/suns, and *lights* as stars – both heavenly
      bodies and objects that give spiritual guidance. The suggestion
      is that *Sons* and *daughters* will end in damnation.
123 **kind**   kind one; one who is closely related to me.
124 **sick in health**   spiritually diseased, from being healthy.
130 **reading**   i.e. of religious and moral texts.
140 **purchase**   profit.
141 **hospital**   orphanage.
157 **glass**   image of perfection.

Act V Scene I

Middleton again uses black humour in this scene through the
stage business with the Duke's body, and the presentation first of
Lussurioso's gullibility and then of his growing understanding of
the situation. The various revenge plots among the brothers
become even more complicated, as Ambitioso makes plans to kill
Supervacuo because of the latter's ambitions to supplant him.

 4 **lay**   bet. Also a pun referring to the position of the Duke's body.
 9 **returns**   versions; also, reports on a court writ or order. The
      Michaelmas legal *term* had *eight* days when these were written.
10 **enow**   enough.
11 **single**   alone.
13 **flesh-flies**   These insects lay their eggs in rotting flesh, so are
      an image of those who live on the spoils of the corrupt court.
14 **against**   before, in anticipation of.
19 **politician**   conspirator.
      in hugger-mugger   in secret.
20 **in catastrophe**   as the conclusion to the tragedy (a theatrical
      term).
24–5 **open in as fair faces**   present opportunities as attractive.
26 **paint**   use make-up; appear.
35 **in some loathsome plight**   i.e. drunk.
43 **villain**   Lussurioso ironically calls his father by the same name
      as the Duke called him in II.iii.14.

58 **all the fire** all the flames of hell.

61 **golls** hands.

62 **qush** splash.

68 **bear us out** support our cause.

71 **Sa, sa, sa** expression a fencer uses when making a thrust.

73 **That's a jest** This is more of Vindice's black humour; see Interpretations page 164.

75 **from your names** inappropriate (undeserved) names.

83 Don't speak about anything we intended to do (i.e. kill Piato).

86 **prate** talk, chatter.

90 **raiment** clothes.

98 **gealed in blood** covered in congealed blood.

102 **clearest** most free from suspicion. This is ironic, as Vindice will later reveal his own guilt.

107 **H'as lost; he may** since he has lost, he can (call me *slave*).

112 **quits him with like terms** repays him with similar names.

115 **prodigious comet** Ambitioso ironically anticipates the comet that appears in V.iii. These were considered to be bad omens, especially for rulers, so could be expected to appear at the death of the Duke.

118 **owes** owns.
    habit outfit.

120 **these clothes** i.e. someone wearing these clothes.

125 **Old dad, dead** See Note to I.ii.82.

126 **cast** rejected.

128 **tug in the new stream** row in the new current (i.e. work with the new circumstances).

134 **that fellow** i.e. Piato.

141 **stick** keep quiet. Again this is ironic, given Vindice's later admission.

148 **something bold** somewhat eager.

157 **feet... twelves** size 9 feet and size 12 tongues. Their tongues, used for flattery, are larger than their feet.

159 **shine** This is a reference to a successful reign by Lussurioso. However, his early death is ironically predicted by the *shine* of the blazing star (V.iii).

173 **revels** masques, a popular form of court entertainment with elaborate costumes, scenery and music. Masks were worn to present a short narrative drama, followed by general

entertainment. These would be appropriate to celebrate Lussurioso's succession, but first there ought to be a decent period of mourning for the old Duke; hence Vindice's disgusted repetition of the word.

several falls   different kinds of events or experiences.

176 **foully bent**   inclined towards vice.

184 **out**   left out.

Act V Scene II

Middleton includes this untypically military scene for several reasons. It reveals that a rebellion has been planned; it shows Vindice as a respected leader; it confirms that he and others regard this public revenge as just. These factors will influence the audience in their judgement of him in the final scene.

1 **of**   made of.

3 **flow in too much milk**   are too soft and pampered.

  have faint livers   lack courage.

7 **Wind up**   stir up.

10 **toward**   imminent.

13 **affect**   desire.

17 **undistinguished hair**   tiniest detail.

19 **a strain or two**   a few musical chords.

27 **drunk down**   made too drunk to resist.

28 **five hundred gentlemen**   This is probably an exaggeration to boost their confidence.

Act V Scene III

The denouement of the play presents the usual conclusion to a revenge drama in that it ends in a bloodbath. Nevertheless, moments of dark humour are created, centred on Vindice, to relieve the tension. Perhaps the final revenge of the play is that of God, who wreaks the vengeance predicted by the comet with the destruction of the entire corrupt dynasty.

Middleton offers no clear judgement on the protagonist and leaves the audience to make their own decisions. The ending of the play is ambiguous; do you regard it as optimistic or pessimistic?

1 sd   The scene opens with two dumb shows. Players would exit after the coronation then re-enter for the banquet.
      blazing star   Middleton's audience would recognize this as an ominous symbol, and dramatic irony would be created if at first the characters seemed unaware of it; see line 5.

5   **That shine**   i.e. the warmth of ducal favour expressed in a *smile* (line 6).

7   **incontinent**   promiscuous.

10   **subsidies**   taxes, penalties.

11   **else 't had**   otherwise it would have.

14   **Beshrew**   curse.

19   **bushing**   with a tail (like a comet).

21   **Before it**   i.e. before the coronation.

22   **whom art and learning weds**   those in whom skill and knowledge meet.

23   **wear locks**   have long hair. The blazing tail of a comet was thought to look like streaming hair.

24   **read**   well-read, learned.

31   **threescore**   sixty. A *score* is 20.

48   For the theatrical imagery in this important line, see Interpretations page 153.

49 sd   **start out of their measure**   are so shocked that they stop their dance. This offers an opportunity for comic staging.

53   **sped**   killed.

61   **wake**   i.e. bring tears to.

68   **Law you now**   really, do you say so (an expression of disbelief).

73   New material to enjoy; I cannot express my feelings. (Presumably those feelings are of grim satisfaction.)

79   **Tell nobody**   What is the effect of this line? Does it have a different resonance by the end of this scene?

83 **unlikely** unpromising.
85 **silver age** See Note to IV.i.35.
89 **quited** repaid.
93 **carried** carried out, managed.
105 **Is't come about** has our luck changed (as the wind does); also, is it really happening.
110–11 See IV.ii.210.
112 **tongueless brass** a silent brass tomb.
113 **died an ass** remained forever ignorant.
115 **sentence** proverb, saying.
118 **witch** prophet, fortune-teller.
120 **been slipped** passed unnoticed.
121 **list** wished.
nobles clipped This is a pun on clipping the edges of gold coins called *nobles*, and the beheading (or at least ruining) of those lords who plotted.
123 **bleed** This is part of the blood imagery of the play; an image of sacrifice may be implied.
124 **turned** i.e. turned back to virtue.
125 **nest of dukes** This metaphor uses the collective noun for a colony of snakes, suggesting that the dukes are poisonous and evil – see Interpretations page 215.
adieu I commend you to God.

Interpretations

Middleton's use of sources

Thomas Middleton, like much of his audience, would have read William Painter's two volumes entitled *The Palace of Pleasure* (1566 and 1575), a series of lurid tales based on translations of Italian writers, describing violent and scandalous events in Italy and Spain. Other Italian events may also have provided material for Middleton, for example the sexual entrapment and assassination of Alessandro de Medici in 1537 (see Further Reading page 232). An Italian or Spanish setting in English Renaissance drama signalled to the audience that this was a place where bloodshed, tyranny, acts of lust and all that was shocking to puritanical minds could be expected.

Middleton probably also drew on his studies of classical history, especially the Roman historian Livy's account of an event that occurred in Rome in the sixth century BCE: Lucretia, wife of an army general, was raped by Sextus, son of the Roman king Tarquin the Proud. She killed herself in despair. This tragedy exacerbated public hostility to the ruling dynasty and triggered an uprising, resulting in the expulsion of the ruling family and the formation of a republic. There is a clear parallel with events in *The Revenger's Tragedy*.

Middleton's worldview in *The Revenger's Tragedy*

The society that Middleton presents in *The Revenger's Tragedy* is spiritually and morally corrupt, ruled by despots driven by lust and greed. On the surface there seems to be little hope of individual self-fulfilment, or moral salvation; but is there evidence of a moral frame against which evil actions will be judged so that human and divine justice can be achieved?

A conventional revenge tragedy would end with the restoration of social order, brought about by the revenger sacrificing himself and purging evil; the hope of redemption and salvation would be affirmed. But Middleton is ambiguous about this. He supplies the morality elements (see page 153) with the parade of deadly sins, the Vice figure as tempter, and several temptation scenes: Vindice tempts Gratiana and Castiza (II.i) and Castiza tempts her mother (IV.iv).

There are clearly 'good' and 'bad' characters. Castiza, whose name means 'chastity', and Gratiana ('grace'), together with Antonio's wife, represent virtuous Christianity. Gratiana's temporary fall and redemption is a miniature model of the Christian scheme of humankind's journey to salvation. Castiza reminds the audience of the presence of the devil when she mentions *hell* (II.i.8). In contrast, the Duke knows he has sinned (II.iii.123–131) but continues to rule with his corrupt regime over a society where innocence is lost and vice prevails.

The ambiguous figure of Vindice is part of both worlds; he is the Vice character in his temptations, yet it is he who reminds the audience of the presence of angels (II.i.137, 241), and who speaks devoutly of *that eternal eye/ That sees through flesh and all* (I.iii.66–67). He further suggests the existence of divine justice when he wonders why heaven does not intervene: *Why does not heaven turn black, or with a frown/ Undo the world?* (II.i.250–251); *Has not heaven an ear? Is all the lightning wasted?* (IV.ii.160). Yet Vindice turns these appeals to heaven into jokes about the theatrical devices that create thunder: *There it goes!* (IV.ii.202); *Dost know thy cue, thou big-voiced crier?* (V.iii.43). However, even the *blazing star* (V.iii), which should be a Christian symbol of renewal, is dismissed by Lussurioso and his nobles as mere superstition.

Does the ending of the play confirm a moral framework? As the revengers caper, Lussurioso's words that they will *dance next in hell* (V.iii.41) sound prophetic. The appearance of Antonio as ruler at the end of the play raises complex issues. He is a good man who has been wronged, yet he was perhaps cowardly in leaving revenge for the assault on his wife to others. It might seem hypocritical of him to condemn Vindice and Hippolito as they, like him, have just claims to revenge. He seems most concerned about his own personal safety: *You that would murder him would murder me* (V.iii.104).

The overall impression given by the play is that of a doomed society rushing to hell (*hurry, hurry, hurry!*, II.i.203), while savouring each *bewitching minute* (III.v.74). Do we pity the characters? Should the drama be taken as a warning? Vindice claims that *When thunder claps, heaven likes the tragedy* (V.iii.48), yet Middleton asks his audiences to make their own decisions.

Activity

Explore the effects Middleton creates with the supernatural elements in *The Revenger's Tragedy*.

Discussion

The Revenger's Tragedy can be read as an allegory of Christian salvation and also as a naturalistic account of a corrupt society. The audience accept the realism of the society that Middleton presents onstage; his characters are recognizable types, and their behaviour is logical and believable within the context of the play.

Thunder is conventionally used as a supernatural element in the revenge tragedy genre, usually as a warning of God's displeasure. In some plays, such as *The Spanish Tragedy, Hamlet* and *The Duchess of Malfi*, the device of a ghost is used to suggest a frame of reference beyond human life, perhaps giving a promise of redemption and salvation. These apparitions work on the minds of protagonists, triggering some sort of reaction.

But Middleton's use of the supernatural reverses the conventional pattern. As mentioned above, Vindice twice seeks divine support for his condemnation of wicked actions (II.i.250 and IV.ii.160). This support seems to be granted by the sound of thunder at IV.ii.202 and V.iii.42. But Vindice's responses are curious; in the first case, he makes what sounds like a flippant response with *There it goes.*

The second response is more explicit, and Middleton breaks the conventions of theatrical illusion and allegory by drawing attention to typical stage devices (*Mark, thunder!/ Dost know thy cue, thou big-voiced crier?,* V.iii.42–43). The audience are forced to consider the play as an artificial creation, and the tense mood is disrupted by the revenger's dark humour. Why would the playwright do this? Is he reminding the audience that they, too, are being asked to judge what they see?

When Vindice adds *When thunder claps, heaven likes the tragedy* (V.iii.48), the theatrical register is evident in the trio *claps, heaven* (in a Jacobean playhouse the stage roof was known as the 'heavens') and *tragedy.* Might this be an appeal to the audience to applaud this tragic drama? Vindice might well speak directly to his audience from the liminal part of the stage (the front border), appealing on Middleton's behalf for public approval.

The influence of morality plays

As discussed on pages 14–16, morality plays, Tudor interludes and even court masques maintained traditions of theme and presentation that survived intact in Middleton's day. All were dramatized allegories representing the battle between good and evil for the human soul; the Vice figure always had a comic aspect and never triumphed, as good always overcame evil; disguise was a central element; there was spectacle; and the drama was episodic in form. All of these qualities are evident in *The Revenger's Tragedy.*

Middleton overlays these aspects of the morality genre with naturalism and satire. He develops a coherent plot by linking episodes thematically and dramatically, often through satirical repetition (see page 185). He incorporates disguise creatively, as Vindice becomes Piato, who becomes Vindice the malcontent, then Vindice himself again – or does he? Middleton asks whether it is possible for Vindice to serve the interests of others in three episodes in the play (Lussurioso in I.iii and IV.ii, the Duke in III.v), without becoming contaminated in the process. The confusion caused by the presence of two sets of masquers onstage in V.iii underscores this.

The play opens with a conventional morality sequence as Vindice introduces four characters as allegories (see Notes page 121) while they process across the stage. Here, and elsewhere in the course of the drama, Middleton makes the seven deadly sins apparent: pride, covetousness (wrongful or greedy desires), lust, gluttony, anger, envy and sloth (moral apathy or sluggishness).

Pride is evident in the way the ducal family use their despotic power and consider themselves above judgement. All of them show scorn for both divine and social law. Covetousness, the unjust desire for other people's property or rights, is evident too in many of their actions; the Duke admits that he is *covetous of all* (II.iii.129). Lust is one of the main drivers of the plot. Gluttony is alluded to in the many references to food, feasting and drunkenness, such as Spurio's reference to *The sin of feasts, drunken adultery* (I.ii.189). All the major characters display anger, even Hippolito in his *Stamping* on the dying Duke (III.v.155); Lussurioso's anger clouds his judgement in condemning the First Gentleman at V.i.136–138. Envy is most obvious in Ambitioso and Supervacuo, who plot the death of their step-brother Lussurioso because they envy his position as heir: *We're both ambitious* (III.vi.23). The Duke recognizes their behaviour as *envy with a poor thin cover o'er't* (II.iii.103). Moral sloth characterizes the ducal family; although they are aware of their sinfulness, they nevertheless continue to luxuriate in their vices. This is evident for example in the Duke: *My hairs are white, and yet my sins are green* (II.iii.131); the Duchess: *Why, there's no pleasure sweet but it is sinful* (III.v.202); Spurio: *Best side to us is the worst side to heaven* (III.v.204); and Junior, on trial for rape: *Well then, 'tis done, and it would please me well/ Were it to do again* (I.ii.60–61).

In the opening scene, Vindice holding the skull represents to the audience the medieval emblem of death, and also the conventional *memento mori* (see page 198), warning the audience to take stock of their own lives as they will face death sooner or later. Vindice's opening speech jolts the audience into complicity with him immediately, preparing for the drama to come. It becomes obvious that the procession of the ducal family represents a parade of the damned waiting for judgement; although physically alive, these characters have long been spiritually, emotionally and morally dead. Vindice, as revenger, must purge the evil represented in these characters, even though he will die physically and perhaps spiritually in the process. Morality play meets revenge tragedy here.

Christopher Ecclestone as Vindice in Alex Cox's 2002 film
Revengers Tragedy

Activity

It is often asserted that Middleton is more concerned with presenting vice than virtue in *The Revenger's Tragedy*. What evidence is there for this?

Discussion

This is potentially a huge topic, so it's best to define specific boundaries to your enquiry. You may consider that Vindice and Spurio are central in presenting the attractiveness of vice and sin (see the Activity on page 208), while Castiza and Gratiana are representations of virtue. It would be helpful to explore two or three examples where vice is made to seem necessary and powerfully attractive, and two or three where virtue is promoted. Then consider the effects created by counterpointing sinful behaviour against Christian virtue. Think about how this contrast affects your response to the society presented in the play, and might enable Middleton to achieve his purposes.

You could begin by considering two of Vindice's speeches (such as his arguments at II.i.192–232) and one of Spurio's (I.ii.177–203). Then move on to address Castiza's spirited defiance of sin and insistence on virtue (II.i.1–8, 32–41), and Gratiana's 'redemption' (IV.iv.118–145).

You might then explore the imagery, register, and poetic and rhetorical devices (such as repetition) that Middleton uses. You could analyse the contrasts between the two ways of life that are offered, and the ways in which you are persuaded to judge the morality of society, court and family.

Middleton's methods of characterization incorporate many elements of the morality drama, as discussed on page 153, but he overlays allegory with naturalism to make his characters credible. Castiza, the allegorical embodiment of chastity, is also an individual young woman who reveals her awareness of the threat posed by poverty in this society (II.i.1–8), yet she serves a true allegorical function as an instrument of correction to her brother and her mother, and more generally as an alternative to court morality. Middleton goes further, creating humour in the episode where she *Gives a box o' th' ear to Vindice* (II.i.32).

Middleton presents Vindice as the primary tempter and introduces the medieval dramatic concept of *psychomachia*, the battle between the warring forces of good and evil for the human soul. This is evident where characters have choices between alternative courses of action, for or against sinful ways. This conflict is externalized when the disguised Vindice, as Vice figure and tempter, and Castiza, representing virtue and chastity, vie for their mother's soul in II.i.

Elsewhere Vindice himself is repeatedly tempted by Lussurioso offering gold and promotion (I.iii.86, II.ii.73, IV.ii.115), as is Hippolito (I.iii.29, IV.i.51–53). It is perhaps significant that Vindice is tempted in this way three times, just as Jesus Christ was tempted in biblical accounts. Vindice's remark that gold is the *Indian devil* that will *quickly enter any man* (I.iii.86–87) makes explicit the temptation to submit to evil.

Ironically, the Duke himself is subjected to a form of temptation in Junior's trial scene (I.ii). The Duke initially seems determined to observe the rules of justice, but the Duchess and the sons persuade him to act otherwise. Middleton shows that the Duke has a choice between a virtuous path, suggested by the judges (I.ii.11–16), and an evil one.

The Duke also tempts Vindice, who says the Duke *hires me by price* (III.v.11). Bribery is a constant theme in the play, as the Duchess seduces Spurio with costly gifts (*Many a wealthy letter have I sent him,/ Swelled up with jewels*, I.ii.111–112), and Ambitioso and Supervacuo attempt to bribe the gaolers with promises of promotion (*if we live to be,/ You shall have a better office*, III.iii.24–25). These other examples of temptation parody the experience of Vindice, who is forced into the role of tempter by his status as revenger, and subjected to temptations because of his poverty and relative powerlessness. The intentions of the other tempters are purely evil, even when they are humorously presented, and this serves to emphasize the comparative purity of Vindice's motives.

The Revenger's Tragedy is therefore grounded in conventions the audience knew and respected from traditional morality plays, while offering implicit comparisons and combining this with biting satire. The result is a play that seems both contemporary and universal, shot through with irony, farce and black humour.

Satire in *The Revenger's Tragedy*

Satirical poetry in Middleton's time was disrespectfully outspoken, and its critics were outraged by its profanity, blasphemy and persuasion to rebellion (see page 16). While entertaining readers with its mockery, satire was intended to expose injustices and to criticize individual and social flaws, especially hypocrisy and lapses of morals. There was usually a genuine contempt for the vices denounced, and a pessimistic view of the prospect for any remedies or improvements. Middleton read and practised writing such poems while studying at Oxford, gaining experience crucial to his three great plays.

There were satirical elements in Elizabethan drama, and the most important influence on Middleton in this regard seems to have been the plays of Ben Jonson and John Marston. The character of Mosca in Jonson's *Volpone* is similar to Vindice in that he is a consummate schemer who is caught in his own trap because he so loves to show off his ingenuity. Yet, significantly, Middleton turns Vindice's situation into a tragedy of the human condition as Vindice has been cheated of his rights by a tyrannical Duke (see page 168). From Marston, Middleton borrowed the concept of the 'malcontent', the central disaffected character, alienated from his society, who acts as commentator for the audience.

In *The Revenger's Tragedy* Middleton uses the three central vehicles of satire: irony, parody and farce. Vindice is the main mouthpiece for satirical language with a serious moral purpose, while the actions of the evil court characters create satirical situations and bring about the ironic reversals that form the structure of the play.

Irony

The play's central pattern of ironic reversals (see page 16) reveals humanity's essential helplessness without a moral framework or divine guidance. Plans go awry and intentions are thwarted; it is the sin of pride that misleads the characters into thinking they can achieve their ambitions through scheming and treachery. This serious message is conveyed with a great deal of black humour.

For example, irony is evident in the way Vindice reveals himself as a murderer three times: the first time is sinister (III.v.166), the second is mocking (V.iii.77), and the third is both foolish and fatal (V.iii.95–97). Middleton offers a brilliant and climactic reversal of fortune as, despite having been saved from blame, the hubristic and irrational Vindice boasts of his guilt. Perhaps Vindice believes that he deserves praise for securing, with Hippolito, revenge for Antonio's wife and the purging of the state; the audience are reminded that this is not the way such a society works.

Perhaps one of the greatest ironies may be found in Vindice's comment after his hiring by Lussurioso: *I've eaten noble poison* (I.iii.167). These words contain the insight that one of the ruling family seems to have loosened the demon in Vindice. But several meanings are evident; should the emphasis be placed on the word *noble* rather than *poison*? Is Vindice a martyr who dies to preserve his own integrity and for the public good?

Acting as commentary for the audience, Vindice's asides and apparently throw-away remarks are often full of ironies, as in his reassuring comment to Lussurioso about the attempted corruption of Castiza, *He shall surely die that did it* (IV.ii.138). The *he* is intended to be understood as Piato, and in fact refers to Lussurioso; but it also implicates Vindice himself, who played the role of Piato and will indeed die for his actions.

Parody

In this highly satirical play, Middleton presents a parody of revenge tragedy, of other contemporary dramas, and of theatrical conventions.

The revenge tragedy is parodied through the effect of dramatic excess: there are so many revengers (seven), and only two of them are justified in the eyes of the audience (Vindice and Hippolito). By the end of Act I, four revenges are pledged: the two just ones are parodied by the two unjust ones of the Duchess and Spurio (against the Duke). In later scenes, desires for revenge multiply, including: Spurio on Lussurioso; Ambitioso and Supervacuo on two targets, Lussurioso and Spurio; and Lussurioso on the disguised Vindice (Piato) as well as on the Duchess and Spurio. The different groups contain both pursuers and pursued, resulting in mayhem as the various would-be revengers criss-cross each other's paths and get in each other's way.

This leads to farce and rich situational irony. For example, Lussurioso storms into the Duchess's chamber intending to catch Spurio in bed with her (II.iii) at the same time as Spurio is trying to catch Lussurioso himself bedding Castiza. Unfortunately for both parties, the Duchess is sleeping with the Duke. Both are confounded. Even Vindice, the arch-revenger, blunders here. The wonder of the situation is that the Duke and Lussurioso both survive long enough to be murdered by Vindice.

The language of revenge plays is unexpectedly subverted in Spurio's vivid colloquialisms, *What makes my dad speak now?* (I.ii.82), and *Old dad, dead?* (V.i.125). Often an audience will laugh out loud, but this crass and inappropriate language reminds us that Spurio is the illegitimate parody of a nobleman. Lussurioso's brief instruction to Vindice, *beg, leg!* (II.ii.72) may also entertain the audience, yet it gives a vivid picture of the way the heir treats his hireling as if he were a dog, unworthy of any rights.

There is also a parody of Shakespeare's tragic hero, Hamlet (1601). This sensitive and introspective character, who would rather philosophize than exact violent revenge, is replaced by Vindice, who is perfectly capable of violence but simply cannot keep his mouth shut – a characteristic that ultimately condemns him to death. While Vindice's broodings, like Hamlet's, have a metaphysical basis and are concerned with the conflict between good and evil in his situation (*Forgive me, heaven*, II.ii.96), Vindice's focus is on the morality of his society, especially in sexual matters. For example, he gives powerful descriptions of various immoral sexual encounters in II.ii.131–146. Some readers would claim that while he is initially moved by a noble desire for justice, Vindice becomes absorbed in his disgust for such conduct and in the cunning of his own schemes: *O 'twill be glorious/ To kill 'em doubled, when they're heaped* (II.iii.3–4).

Middleton also parodies theatrical conventions, for example when the use of stage thunder is undercut by comments from Vindice that draw attention to its artificiality (IV.ii.202, V.iii.42–43). Middleton also gives several theatrical metaphors to his protagonist, such as calling Gloriana's skull a *property* that *shall bear a part/ E'en in it own revenge* (III.v.100–101) and commenting that *When the bad bleeds, then is the tragedy good* (III.v.199). In these remarks and in his references to disguise, Vindice reminds the audience that they are in a theatre; the comic effect masks a serious prompt to make judgements on what is being presented.

Farce

The play contains several episodes that have a very absurd and farcical effect. The Duke and Duchess are unexpectedly discovered in bed together (II.iii); Ambitioso and Supervacuo are gloating over a severed head that they believe is Lussurioso's when he enters to thank them for saving his life (III.vi). Here as elsewhere, farce is triggered by the traditional means of mistaken identity. When Ambitioso and Supervacuo realize that their plot to free their younger brother and to have their step-brother executed has totally backfired, the situation and the ensuing fast-paced dialogue are comic, but the diabolical references (*furies!/ Plagues! Confusions! Darkness! Devils!*, III.vi.75–76) nevertheless remind onlookers of the true nature of the Duchess's sons. Retribution for sin occurs independently of human wishes.

Lussurioso features again in this type of black comedy when he is duped over the apparent murder of Piato (V.i). One of the key moments of this episode is Lussurioso's boastful *Puh, am I a lord for nothing, think you?* (V.i.69); followed by the stage direction *Vindice and Hippolito stab the corpse, which falls forward* and Vindice's mimetic comment *Thump, there he lies.* The dramatic irony is taken further as Lussurioso is painfully slow to realize the truth, but when he recognizes that *'Tis the old duke my father*, Vindice's nonchalant response is *That's a jest* (V.i.73). It is indeed a jest, at Lussurioso's expense, but also ultimately at the expense of the protagonist himself, who becomes the victim of his own ready wit.

A final farcical moment occurs when the second set of masquers realize that their murderous plans have been anticipated by an even more ruthless set of murderers (V.iii.49). The masquers' attempt to kill men who are already dead parallels the earlier situation where Vindice stabs the corpse of the Duke. Death itself becomes farcical.

Vindice shows awareness that he is living through a farcical situation when he comments to Hippolito *I'm hired to kill myself* (IV.ii.207). Apart from providing opportunities for some very ingenious plotting, this statement touches upon more serious issues about the abuse of power (see page 204). Vindice's comments often humorously point up the farcical aspects of a scene, for example when he asks Hippolito to stay *With the bony lady* (III.v.121), or when he speaks to the Duke of her: *Sh'as somewhat a grave look with her* (136–137). The black humour nevertheless reminds an audience of the grotesque and painful nature of what they are seeing.

Perhaps the cruellest moment of farce is Vindice's final exchange with the dying Lussurioso, culminating with the command to *Tell nobody* (V.iii.79). This mental torture is masked, in line with court convention, with black humour. Clearly, Middleton is a master satirist; but it is important to bear in mind that his comedy never serves the function of light relief; arising as it does directly from the actions of the play, the black humour heightens the audience's sense of the evil presented onstage.

Activity

Analyse Middleton's methods of creating satirical humour and farce in one scene.

Discussion

In the case of III.vi, where Ambitioso and Supervacuo will realize that Junior has been executed in a case of mistaken identity, Middleton splits the scene into two parts. In the first part (lines 1–54), the audience are amused by the dramatic irony of the brothers' lavishly self-congratulatory mood as each claims responsibility for their 'success', then pretends, in front of the Officer, to feel grief. The mood dramatically changes at line 55, with the entrance of Lussurioso and the simple exclamation O. This leads to a comic sequence of exclamations in his presence, modulating to a series of curses after his exit. These are heightened by punctuation and the sharing of verse lines between the two brothers.

Characterization

In *The Revenger's Tragedy* Middleton creates characters that operate on three levels: allegorically, naturalistically and dramatically. In the first case their function is to suggest a moral frame beyond the social world presented on stage. On the naturalistic level, their actions and dialogue reveal the issues that arise in this society. Their dramatic functions relate to the development of the plot and the way that the playwright jolts the audience into making judgements.

Vindice

Middleton presents Vindice as the allegorical Vice figure (see pages 15 and 153). This means that he has a dramatic profile as the tempter, the intermediary who connects with the audience,

163

and the main agent for plot development. As a malcontent, Vindice is introspective, offering biting analysis of contemporary social problems. As the revenger, he will be the purger of evil, both in corrupt individuals and the state.

The structure of the play suggests that Vindice's acts of revenge are morally justified; the Duke poisoned his betrothed and Lussurioso intended to corrupt his sister. When wreaking vengeance on the Duke he claims that *heaven is just* (III.v.182). With Hippolito, Vindice will also avenge the death of Antonio's wife. The audience can sympathize with Vindice's plans and deeds, yet Middleton parodies these legitimate grievances with those of the corrupt ducal family, such as the Duchess's (I.ii.107) and Spurio's (I.ii.177). Similarly, Vindice's judgements of his mother and sister (II.i) are parodied in Ambitioso and Supervacuo's condemnation of their mother, the Duchess (IV.iii.9–14).

We are drawn to Vindice by his quick thinking (for example at II.ii.159–161 and IV.ii.203), compared to the stupidity of the nobles; and he provides much of the humour of the play through his rapid improvisation (as in I.iii) and his wit: *I'm hired to kill myself* (IV.ii.207); *Sh'as somewhat a grave look with her* (III.v.136–137).

He is intelligent and clear-thinking, and in harsh words summarizes one of the main issues of the play, the use of disguise: *See, ladies, with false forms/ You deceive men, but cannot deceive worms* (III.v.96–97). His poetry enriches the texture of the play, for example in his graphic account of a lecherous society (II.ii.131–146), in which he conveys the pace of a heedless rush towards doom, *apace, apace, apace, apace!*, echoing his earlier *hurry, hurry, hurry!* (II.i.203).

Initially, Vindice represents those deprived of their rightful place in society because of their fathers' folly or misfortune, and the injustices of a despotic ruler (I.i.124–127); he is forced into corrupt service, like his brother. His honour as the head of a family and as a brother has been denied by the actions of the Duke and Lussurioso; in this society there is no respect for individuals. His comments on female vanity relate the world of the play to society at large, where *many an infant starves* (III.v.85). The skull of Gloriana is a symbol of his promise to avenge the dead; her name reminds the audience of a past golden age (see page 200). In these ways, Vindice claims our sympathies; does he retain them?

Early in the play, Vindice shows that he is all too aware of the moral dilemmas he faces. He is troubled by the necessity of shaming his mother in his comments about her to Lussurioso, but the alternative is to fall from grace by telling lies: *Now must I blister my soul, be forsworn,/ Or shame the woman that received me first* (II.ii.36–37). Some readers suggest that he changes as the play progresses, becoming entrapped in his own ingenious schemes, and that he loses his moral bearings. Is this a fair assessment? He often rejoices in his own cunning and ingenuity, which he confidently believes will keep him from being suspected of the Duke's murder; he will be *the clearest man* (V.i.102), and will perfect his plotting with further murders: *Strike one strain more, and then we crown our wit* (V.i.180). Throughout the play Vindice indicates that he has a belief in redemption and salvation (see page 151), but when he takes on the disguise of Piato (meaning 'hidden' or 'empty'), saying *Am I far enough from myself?* (I.iii.1), and later admits *I've eaten noble poison* (I.iii.167), has he begun to change? It is worth noting, however, that Vindice subsequently drops the disguise and appears under his own name.

Vindice relishes the opportunity for long-awaited revenge (*I'm in a throng of happy apprehensions*, III.v.30), but does he go to extremes with his plans of murder? The cruelty of the Duke's death raises questions, but could it be that the eyelids the murderers *tear* open and the tongue pierced by the dagger represent the eyes and lips that initiated the offence against Gloriana? This scene is the only one in the play where Hippolito seems shocked at Vindice's behaviour (*Why, brother, brother!*, III.v.49) – or is his exclamation one of admiration for Vindice's ingenuity? Has the punishment been finely calculated to fit the crime? Or has the role of Piato, which Vindice assumed he could shake off at will (*I'll put on that knave for once*, I.i.93) taken him over? Vindice eventually does get rid of his disguise as Piato, however, and does not go beyond his planned revenge murders; the final bloodbath is triggered by the Duchess's sons.

Vindice seems to be acknowledging guilt when he includes himself in the comment *Villains all three* (III.v.152); *we are all mad people* (III.v.79), he claims. Later, he seems to accept Lussurioso's characterization of him as *villain* and *slave pander* when he responds, ironically, *All this is I* (IV.ii.123, 129, 132). Is he admitting that he too has been lost to sin? When Vindice arranges with his co-conspirators to impersonate the masquers (who turn out to be murderers too) in the minutest detail (V.ii.15–17), is Middleton implying that all are alike in their evil?

Throughout the play Middleton presents the idea of transformation (see page 182); is Vindice subject to this? Hippolito does not think so; as Vindice abandons the Piato persona, he comments *y'are yourself* (IV.ii.1). Vindice, who earlier reminded the audience of the presence of the *eternal eye* (I.iii.66), seems to be consistent in his outrage at the nobility's lack of concern over the Duke's death (V.i.173), yet his heartlessness in blaming the innocent Fourth Man for Lussurioso's murder (V.iii.69) is startling.

In the revenge tragedy genre, the revenger usually dies in his efforts to purge the original offence; has Vindice committed what amounts to spiritual suicide? Middleton leaves open the final judgement on Vindice. Certain that he has cleansed and renewed the state, endorsing Hippolito's view that Antonio is *the hope/ Of Italy* (V.iii.83–84), he ironically reveals his guilt to Antonio. He seems to expect acknowledgement for achieving revenge, including revenge for the death of Antonio's wife, and for purging the corrupt state: *Thou hast no conscience: are we not revenged?* (V.iii.107). Does Middleton's use of the word *conscience* imply that Antonio is misjudging the situation? Does it suggest that Vindice believes in the purity of his own motives? He is forced to admit that *'Tis time to die, when we are ourselves our foes* (V.iii.109), possibly because he has made such a grave miscalculation about the situation.

Readers point out that there is no direct reference to repentance, redemption or salvation at the end of the play (but see the Activity on page 214). Is Vindice too realistic, or cynical, to expect this? Is he a martyr, or a disillusioned victim? Is he a noble warrior for justice, or contaminated and corrupt? Compared to the ducal family, Vindice is a just man with a just aim; but he has committed two murders. Has the audience become so dazzled by Vindice's virtuosity that Antonio's cold, logical judgement is a call back to reality? Middleton leaves the decision to you.

Activity

Discuss Vindice's role in the context of the revenge tragedy genre.

Discussion

The genre includes several characteristics that are evident in Middleton's play. There is the traditional five-act plot development; there is a court setting in Italy, and one or more revengers; the revengers challenge the power of a tyrannical despot, if necessary sacrificing themselves for the common good. Middleton does not include the usual supernatural trappings such as a ghost, but there is thunder and a blazing star, which might hint at a higher power.

The Jacobean audience would have conflicting responses to a revenger such as Vindice, because although violent revenge was forbidden by law, it was popularly approved in specific circumstances, such as when wrong was committed but the victim could not secure legal redress, when the injury was carried out in a treacherous or dishonourable manner, or when revenge was sought on behalf of relatives by blood or marriage. Vindice's revenge on the Duke for the murder of his betrothed Gloriana, and on Lussurioso for the attempts to corrupt his sister Castiza, clearly meets all three conditions; an audience would be unwilling to condemn Vindice on these grounds.

Middleton presents the two just revengers, Vindice and Hippolito, conventionally bearing the sword of justice (l.iii.171 and l.iv.57). Vindice speaks the conventional language of the revenger: *Vengeance, thou murder's quit-rent... O keep thy day, hour, minute, I beseech* (l.i.39–41). He claims his motive is just and supported by heaven (III.v.182). Opportunity for revenge (I.i.55) comes with his service to Lussurioso, and when he is asked to act as bawd for the Duke (III.v). There are the conventional delays before the acts of revenge are carried out (II.ii.91–93, V.i.16–22), and when he is about to triumph, Vindice's tone is that of the archetypal revenger: *Now nine years' vengeance crowd into a minute!* (III.v.122).

Some critics detect a change in Vindice's attitude in the closing couplet of the scene in which he murders the Duke: *The dukedom wants a head, though yet unknown: / As fast as they peep up, let's cut 'em down* (III.v.219–220). Some believe this speech marks a deterioration in Vindice's judgement, but there is another view. With one personal revenge completed, Vindice moves on to accomplish the revenger's second task: to purge the corruption of the state and restore order. He does not seem to stray beyond this wider task.

Middleton complicates the revenge tragedy with the frequent use of satire (see page 158). One of the most important of these moments is when the revenger confesses in a surprising way (V.iii.97). Perhaps Middleton wishes to query the ethics of revenge? Perhaps he wants to suggest something about the validity of the revenge tragedy genre?

The Duke

In the opening line of the play, Middleton introduces the Duke as an allegorical figure of evil: *Duke – royal lecher! Go, gray-haired adultery*. Vindice's powerful description places the Duke in the audience's eyes as *A parched and juiceless luxur* (I.i.9). He has poisoned his dukedom not only with his own vices but with his misuse of power, as in his treatment of Vindice's father: *The duke did much deject him* (I.i.124). Vindice represents the consequences of the Duke's despotic rule. Because of the treatment of his father he has lost his place in society, and his rights as the fiancé of Gloriana have been outraged; shortly the Duke's son will also deny his familial rights over Castiza. It is indeed a type of justice that the Duke's desire for illicit sex becomes his downfall (III.v).

We are twice shown the Duke's lack of concern for the workings of justice. He is persuaded by his wife to suspend Junior's sentence of death, despite the judges' harsh account of his crime (I.ii); he prefers to put off the judgement to another day. Similarly, despite Lussurioso's potentially traitorous attack on him, the Duke plays with the idea of justice in order to test Ambitioso and Supervacuo, but then announces *We freely pardon him* (II.iii.121).

Although there is no development of it, the Duke's character is fleshed out sufficiently to provide credibility in the plot. He is no fool; he sees through the insincerity of his stepsons (*Here's envy with a poor thin cover o'er't*, II.iii.103), and he reveals a shocking self-knowledge in the face of possible death: *O, take me not in sleep; I have great sins* (II.iii.9). Directors sometimes use his cowardly terror as an opportunity for humour, but his soliloquy at the end of this scene also shows sober self-knowledge.

Dramatically, the Duke's death is a central gruesome spectacle in the play. But he remains largely a type, a tyrannical ruler to whom no sympathy can be given, and who helps to weigh the balance of the audience's judgements in favour of Vindice.

Lussurioso

Lussurioso's name defines him allegorically as Lust, and he is *as impious steeped as* his father the Duke (I.i.2). Again there is little development from this type. All his actions signify his corruption, and he denies Vindice his right as head of a household to protect his sister, Castiza. In his role as intermediary to the audience, Vindice testifies to Lussurioso's uncontainable lust:

> I know his heat is such,
> Were there as many concubines as ladies
> He would not be contained, he must fly out.

> (I.i.82–84)

Lussurioso openly admits that *I am past my depth in lust,/ And I must swim or drown* (I.iii.89–90).

Middleton shows him operating within a culture of bribery and corruption, seen in his offer to Vindice: *What office couldst thou be ambitious for?* (II.ii.73). He claims to feel distress on his father's death, but his aside is eloquent about his true feelings: *Welcome, sweet titles!* (V.i.153). His immediate actions on his succession to the dukedom reveal his priorities:

That foul, incontinent duchess we have banished;
The bastard shall not live...
      he and the stepsons
Shall pay their lives for the first subsidies.

V.iii.7–10

Lussurioso is not only utterly pitiless but impious, happy to allow a drunkard to *reel to hell* (V.i.56).

In a lighter vein, Middleton offers an amusing vignette of Lussurioso's vanity in selecting as his favourite the courtier who wishes he *shall ne'er die* (V.iii.34); the audience would recognize the implied criticism of James I's habit of promoting personal favourites. Hippolito places Lussurioso for our judgement with the reference to *his secretary the devil* (IV.ii.9), and like his father Lussurioso is brazen in his vice: *It is our blood to err* (I.iii.73). The word *blood* signifies that it is a family trait, and this denial of

Eddie Izzard as Lussurioso, Marc Warren as Supervacuo in Alex Cox's 2002 film *Revengers Tragedy*

personal responsibility suggests that he sees such excess as the right of rulers. His selfishness and indifference to the rights of others condemn him in the eyes of the audience, gaining sympathy for Vindice as revenger.

Activity

What is the dramatic function of Lussurioso?

Discussion

Middleton layers the morality-type figure of Lussurioso with sufficient characterization to make him credible as a flesh-and-blood character in the drama, yet uses him as a device to bind together the two elements of Vindice's revenge. His lust for Castiza leads to Vindice's employment at court; his revelation that Castiza is his target leads to a dramatic moment in the play where Vindice is wrong-footed for once (I.iii.125). This in turn leads to Vindice's opportunity to serve the Duke.

Dramatically, Lussurioso promotes different moods in the play; his ruthlessness and lust are chilling, yet several comic effects centre on him. He is involved in at least four moments of black humour: his error in bursting into the Duchess's bedroom (II.iii); his sudden entrance when his step-brothers believe they are looking at his severed head (III.vi.55); his excitable lies to Vindice about his rejection of Piato (IV.ii.156–158); and Vindice's whisper to him as he is dying, *Tell nobody* (V.iii.79).

Spurio

Spurio is described as the Duke's *bastard true-begot in evil* (I.i.3). In this character, Middleton draws together the morality convention and that of Elizabethan drama, where the illegitimate son is isolated and bitter because he lacks rights to property, and even to respect. Spurio's name means 'false' or 'illegitimate'. Middleton uses him to hint at the immorality of the court of James I, where illegitimate sons were openly acknowledged and sometimes made legitimate heirs. This threatened the stable inheritance system, which had been the basis of feudal society.

Middleton presents Spurio as a foil to Vindice; unlike the other 'bad' characters, he is given energy and vitality. He too is a revenger who claims *My revenge is just* (I.ii.190), and he too is socially disadvantaged. As the Duchess maliciously makes clear, the circumstances of his birth have cut him off from great privileges, *For had he* (the Duke) *cut thee a right diamond,/ Thou hadst been next set in the dukedom's ring* (I.ii.149–150).

Spurio has a powerful command of language, as is evident in his soliloquy at the end of I.ii, a superb set-piece that rivals Vindice's eloquence; he, too, prowls restlessly around the edges of society.

But there are significant differences between him and Vindice. The latter is a just revenger with faith in a divine scheme, while Spurio claims to be of the devil's party (O, *I'd a hot-backed devil to my father*, I.ii.164) and seethes with hatred and bitterness. His soliloquy testifies to the drunkenness and immorality that led to his conception, and which is his inheritance. With his dark menace and his choice of adultery and incest as methods of revenge, he again increases the audience's sympathies for Vindice's more justifiable actions.

Spurio lashes out at all of the ducal family: the Duchess, whom he uses to achieve revenge on the Duke (*I love thy mischief well, but I hate thee*, I.ii.193); Lussurioso, whom he plans to kill, saying *I'll damn you at your pleasure* (II.ii.128); and Ambitioso, whom he does kill (V.iii.55). Driven by bitterness towards his whole extended family, his attitude is contrasted to Vindice's concern for his own family. His final efforts to gain revenge parody Vindice's as he, too, plans murder-by-masque. Middleton offers a neat twist here. The audience probably feel they know what's coming, but both sets of revengers are disguised; does Middleton suggest the similarities between them despite earlier differences? Is either murder plan to be condoned? The climactic moment turns to black humour as Spurio's band are caught out trying to kill men already dead, and then they attack each other in their frustration.

Ambitioso, Supervacuo, Junior

The Duchess's three sons also have names that reflect the 'type' they represent. Ambitioso's name indicates his half-concealed ambition to succeed to the dukedom; Supervacuo's name means 'superfluous' or 'unnecessary', which reflects his position as a second son. Middleton uses the youngest, Junior, as a dramatic device to demonstrate the Duke's contempt for justice (I.ii), paralleling this scene with that of Antonio's grief (I.iv). Junior's action in raping Antonio's wife, and the Duke's failure to deal with the situation, lead to both Antonio and the Duchess turning against the Duke.

Junior shows the greatest contempt for the processes of law and justice in his trial scene, and again in III.iv. He believes that he and his brothers are above the law, but his confidence that *I shall not be long a prisoner* (III.iv.22–23) is a dramatic irony. Even facing death, Junior puns on the sexual connotations of *die* (III.iv.86); his character is a harsh vignette of a privileged young man who acts as if justice and religious faith have no relevance to him.

Like Junior, the older brothers have no regard for the law and justice; Supervacuo claims that *The duchess' sons are too proud to bleed* (III.i.21). They represent a satire on corruption at the court of James I; dramatically, they are a source of rich humour. There is not much to distinguish between them, but Supervacuo is slightly more assertive than Ambitioso, as is necessary in a younger son (*Brother, let my opinion sway you once*, III.i.1; *Why, was 't not my invention, brother…* III.vi.5). He is quick to claim succession to the dukedom when Lussurioso is dead, despite Ambitioso's seniority (V.iii.54).

Middleton uses parallel situations to reveal the hypocrisy and corruption of the brothers; first Ambitioso pleads for Junior (I.ii.31–33) and then promises to devise a *trick* to set him free (I.ii.86); then Ambitioso and Supervacuo pretend to plead for Lussurioso while secretly trying to hasten his death in order to become heirs to the dukedom (II.iii); and finally they believe they have tricked officers into executing Lussurioso, but have really sealed the fate of Junior. Middleton presents this as black farce, when the brothers – so confident in their schemes that they have even begun to dispute between themselves who should take the credit – suddenly see Lussurioso, *Alive!/ In health!/ Released?* (III.vi.59). Their disjointed exclamations are split over shared lines of verse for comic effect and for pace: *O death and vengeance!/ Hell and torments!/... O furies!/ Plagues!/ Confusions!/ Darkness!/ Devils!* (III.vi.67–76). Middleton makes their evil clear in all these references to the diabolic forces that they represent.

The revenge plots of Ambitioso and Supervacuo, like those of Spurio, offer an ironic parallel to Vindice's. They too are delayed in their planned revenge on both Spurio (IV.iii.6–7) and Lussurioso (V.i.189–193). Unlike Hippolito and Vindice – brothers who work trustingly and effectively together – these brothers quarrel foolishly (III.vi.1–30). Their shared trait of ruthless ambition (*We're both ambitious, be it our amity*, III.vi.23) apparently unites them but in fact makes them rivals, and leads to their deaths in the parallel masque (V.iii.54–55).

Activity

What is the significance of Junior in *The Revenger's Tragedy?*

Discussion

The character of Junior typifies the author's economy of style in creating multiple effects. Although this youngest brother appears relatively little onstage, he does raise central issues.

Primarily he is a vehicle through which Middleton establishes, at the beginning of the play, the injustices of this society. The efforts of his mother and his brothers to turn aside justice in his trial (I.ii) demonstrate this, but Junior's own arrogance and lack of respect for both law and religion are striking. His contemptuous attitude to women emphasizes the misogyny of this patriarchal court, and his cynicism reveals the lack of value he places on human life. His crime of rape is the primary cause of the second just revenge in the play, that on behalf of Antonio's wife, and his 'mistaken' execution gives rise to some of the most humorous and farcical moments in the play (see page 161).

Hippolito

Hippolito is the younger brother of Vindice (Lussurioso mocks his youth at I.iii.138), and like Vindice he demonstrates the helplessness of impoverished young gentlemen trying to make a living in this society (I.i.62–64). He offers an ironic commentary on the court (*In silk and silver, brother; never braver*, I.i.52), and on Lussurioso (*He and his secretary the devil*, IV.ii.9).

Middleton presents him dramatically, like Vindice, as a just revenger; Hippolito proposes a solemn oath to seek justice for Antonio's wife against an attacker who *was found/ Guilty in heaven* (I.iv.63–64). He shares Vindice's joy at their revenge on the Duke: *Brother, how happy is our vengeance* (V.i.143). He too sees their revenges as both personal and political, calling Antonio *the hope/ Of Italy* (V.iii.83–84.)

Hippolito has an important dramatic function in presenting his brother with the opportunity for revenge through his position at court, and advising him as to the appropriate disguise. Occasionally he gets things wrong, as when he reports the gossip about Spurio (II.ii.109–110), which provides Vindice with a necessary distraction for Lussurioso but causes problems when the latter bursts in to find his father, instead of Spurio, in bed with the Duchess.

Middleton shows Hippolito's closeness to his brother (III.v.4–6) and his ready invention (IV.i.44–46, IV.ii.183–187). He too addresses the audience directly, commenting in a witty aside *An impossible task, I'll swear,/ To bring him hither that's already here* (IV.ii.173–174). Like Vindice, he occasionally employs a theatrical metaphor: in *You flow well, brother* (II.ii.147), the word *flow* refers to the actor's delivery of his lines. Hippolito readily takes part in Vindice's more dubious actions, such as threatening their mother with a dagger in IV.iv, and taking part in the torture of the dying Duke as they stamp on him (III.v.155) and use their daggers to silence him. He both encourages his brother (IV.ii.214) and calms him down (V.i.23–25) as necessary.

Hippolito offers a moral commentary, and is clear-sighted about the way they are drawn into unsavoury activities (*we are both made bawds a new-found way!*, II.ii.16), just as he sees that at court he has been made an *unnatural slave* (II.ii.11). He perhaps shows some anxiety about his brother's actions when he seems to warn Vindice *Nay, brother, you reach out o' th' verge now* (I.iii.17), and when Vindice produces Gloriana's skull, he exclaims *Why, brother, brother!* (III.v.49). Is he anxious about the morality of such actions, or is he ensuring that they don't lose focus on their task? Perhaps the latter exclamation has a different tone, and he is impressed with Vindice's use of the skull; he praises his brother's *constant vengeance*, and perhaps ambiguously the *quaintness* of his *malice* (III.v.107–108).

Although Vindice's dominating presence seems to overshadow him, nevertheless Hippolito is effective as a dramatic device, helping to set up a parallel with the unjust siblings, and supporting Vindice as a committed revenger who believes in the essential justice of their joint undertakings, trapped as they are in a corrupt court and a society steeped in vice.

Activity

Compare and contrast the two sets of siblings in the play.

Discussion

Vindice, Hippolito and Castiza represent the longing for justice and virtue, while Lussurioso, Spurio, Ambitioso, Supervacuo and Junior are all on the side of evil and concerned solely with personal gratification. Through these opposing groups, Middleton represents the battle between good and evil for human souls, and the struggle for a just society against powerful vested interests. How does the play present these conflicts? Think about:

• the language and registers used: the 'good' refer to heaven, grace, virtue, angels; the 'bad' refer to the devil, hell and all kinds of sins

- the different examples of revenge, and the characters' treatment of each other and those dependent on them
- the structure of the play; how do the actions of the ducal brothers reflect on those of Vindice's family?
- why Middleton uses parallel structures
- where the two groups merge, and why
- the outcome of the revenge plots, and the ending of the play – is it optimistic or pessimistic?

Antonio

Antonio is presented rather ambiguously, leaving the audience to judge how suitable he is as a future ruler. Does he represent the just, wise and honourable nobleman who will lead his society to rebirth and renewal, or is he a weak and cowardly old man whose election suggests a bleak view of the future for this society?

To support the first reading, Antonio is free of any link with evil or corruption. He responds graciously to Hippolito's plan for revenging his wife (*Kind gentlemen, I thank you in mine ire*, I.iv.65), but prefers to leave vengeance to heaven: *Just is the law above* (V.iii.90). He takes no part in the conspiracy in V.ii, or in the subsequent murders. He regards the death of Lussurioso and his step-brothers as *A piteous tragedy!* (V.iii.61), and magnanimously makes no judgement on their crimes and corruption, as these have been punished by their deaths. Although Antonio is wrong in his accusation of treason against the Fourth Man (V.iii.70–72), this man is guilty of the murder of Spurio.

Perhaps Antonio sees the murders, especially that of the old Duke, as evidence of the fatal corruption gripping this society: *You that would murder him would murder me* (V.iii.104); they almost cause the collapse of the state. In this situation, Antonio is indeed the *hope/ Of Italy*, the ruler who can bring *the silver age again* (V.iii.83–85). Will his rule be redemptive and bring about the salvation of society, as he says he intends to do (*May I so rule that heaven may keep the crown*, V.iii.88)?

Other aspects of Antonio's role are more ambiguous. Middleton repeatedly stresses Antonio's old age (I.iv.77; V.iii.62, 84–85), which could be taken as emphasizing his wisdom and dignity, or his weakness and his nearness to death. On his first appearance, he is named in the stage direction as *the discontented Lord Antonio* (I.iv); Middleton has Vindice describe his father similarly (I.i.127), and Hippolito characterizes Vindice in these terms to Lussurioso (IV.ii.31). To be *discontented* could be a vice or (in this society) a virtue.

Activity

What evidence is there to suggest that Antonio will not make a strong or just ruler?

Discussion

Antonio might seem cowardly in not becoming personally engaged with avenging his wife, while arguably fuelling the fires of revenge in Hippolito and his companions. Perhaps Middleton presents more serious flaws. When Antonio mistakenly condemns the Fourth Man, there is no mention of any trial: *Away with that foul monster* (V.iii.70). Similarly, Vindice and Hippolito are summarily sentenced to death: *Bear 'em to speedy execution* (V.iii.101). The impulsive and dubious nature of his judgement recalls that of the Duke in relation to Junior (I.ii) and Lussurioso (II.iii). Finally, Antonio appears to condemn the brothers purely out of concern for his own personal safety: *Such an old man as he!/ You that would murder him would murder me* (V.iii.103–104). Is he getting rid of potential opponents to his rule?

These two contrasted readings of Antonio, one offering hope, and the other hopeless, perhaps reflect Middleton's Calvinist background. Calvinism is the set of Protestant religious beliefs developed by John Calvin (1509–1564), according to which God had already chosen the small minority of people who would be saved (the 'elect'). The majority of people were therefore inevitably damned, and no amount of penance or good works could change this judgement. The 'elect' would always be saved and brought to heaven, while the remainder of humankind were depraved in every way, in their thoughts, words and deeds, even if they seemed (and believed themselves to be) virtuous.

Middleton would have first experienced the doctrine of Calvinism through his parish minister, Oxford-educated Thomas Sanderson; Henry Airay, the provost of his Oxford college, Queen's, was a leading evangelical Calvinist, and his wife's grandfather, John Marbeck, had been persecuted for his Calvinism. The young Middleton would have further experience of this doctrine through attending the popular sermons that were given by visiting lecturers. A prominent theme for sermons was the question of how a person would know whether he were among the 'elect', which led to much soul-searching and self-analysis among Calvinists.

Some readers believe that Middleton's Calvinism is shown throughout this play. You might consider this suggestion by exploring how various characters might reflect the idea, and how the ending of the play would correspond with the doctrine.

The Duchess

Women are given small roles in this play, but they help to develop Middleton's themes. The Duchess is defined in the first few lines as someone who *will do with devil* (I.i.4), and she has no redeeming qualities. Her marriage to the Duke seems to have been motivated by her ambition for her three sons, as she has nothing but contempt for *his withered grace* (I.ii.96). She holds justice, too, in contempt as she pleads for her youngest son to go unpunished for rape.

Like her husband she is aware of the existence of a higher moral framework, as she speaks of *the justice/ Of that unbribèd, everlasting law* (I.ii.162–163). But she freely plots *vengeance* by a method that *picks open hell* (I.ii.174–175). Other characters testify to her wicked cunning: Spurio claims to *hate* her but to *love* her *mischief* (I.ii.193); the Duke speaks of her *stepmother's wit* (II.iii.86); and her own children aim to *Learn of our mother; let's dissemble too* (V.i.123).

Her dramatic function is to trigger Spurio's revenge. She represents personal, familial and social corruption.

Castiza

Castiza's name is another instance of the influence of the morality play in Middleton's drama; she is a figure representing Chastity, free of all sin. A saintly character, her judgement of Junior gives support to Vindice's second role as revenger in purging the court of evil: *Royal blood! Monster, he deserves to die,/ If Italy had no more hopes but he* (I.i.112–113).

There is a little development of her character; she humorously highlights the immorality of the court as she spiritedly *Gives a box o' th' ear to Vindice* (II.i.32), displaying contempt for the advances of the Duke's son. She also gives a voice to downtrodden subjects of the Duke (and of James I) who will not accept the general immorality of the court patronage system and are forced to live *low and empty in estate* (II.i.4).

Castiza's role is to anchor the moral and spiritual frame of the play, as she tests her mother in IV.iv, and reminds the audience that the devil, the *wicked one*, is at work in this society (II.i.172, 204). She believes that the devil has possessed her mother: *Mother, come from that poisonous woman there!* (II.i.236). In contrast to the corrupt kisses of the depraved characters, her kiss to her repentant mother is from her *soul* (IV.iv.147).

Gratiana

Like her daughter, Gratiana is an allegorical figure, representing Grace, the moral centre of the play. Initially, Middleton's name for her seems ironic, as she yields so easily to Vindice's temptation and seems willing to sacrifice her daughter's honour in exchange for wealth (II.i.104), ambiguously represented as *angels* (II.i.86–87). But even in this scene Gratiana excites the audience's compassion for the poor subjects of despotic rulers, who must either accept the general corruption and seek favour at court, or sink into poverty.

Gratiana's main allegorical significance is that she represents the workings of Christian grace on the human soul, leading sinners to salvation. The *blessèd dew* (IV.iv.49) of her tears leads to repentance (*O you heavens,/ Take this infectious spot out of my soul*, IV.iv.51–52) and then to redemption, as she muses *I wonder now what fury did transport me!/ I feel good thoughts begin to settle in me* (IV.iv.94–95). Her new resolve is tested by Castiza, and found to be firm. Middleton appears to be suggesting, through Gratiana's fall and rise, that there is a moral and spiritual code available to humankind as an alternative to the general corruption on view elsewhere.

Activity

Analyse the ways in which Middleton uses the device of the soliloquy to reveal character.

Discussion

The dramatic soliloquy usually has two purposes: it allows the character to provide some justification or at least reason for his or her actions, and through direct communication with the audience the character either confirms or alienates their sympathy.

Just as the Duke's soliloquy at II.iii.123–131 is of great importance in his characterization and in presenting the issues of the play, Lussurioso's soliloquy at IV.i.62–72 is similarly revealing.

- He is shown to be petulant and spiteful (62–64).
- The dangers of ducal service are made clear (64–67).
- His contempt for individual subjects and his willingness to exploit their powerlessness are evident (69–72).

- He is shown to be willing to use bribery to corrupt those serving him (71–72).
- His negative register reveals that he regards his subjects as *slaves* (63, 69) who are likely to be full of *black* discontent (70). They are worthless to him, other than for use in his schemes.

Structure and effects

The concept of transformation in political, social, moral and spiritual values unifies all aspects of *The Revenger's Tragedy*. These values were changing in Middleton's society (see pages 7–10), and in the world of the theatre, too, a new system of management and playwriting was evolving. Transformation is similarly central to the staging, setting and dramatic effects that Middleton presents in the play.

Sophisticated Jacobean audiences enjoyed the shocks, the reversals and the multiplications of meaning that emerged from the play in performance. Although the playing space seemed neutral, the stage became a palace, a court of law, a prison, a bedroom, a garden house or a banqueting hall by combining the simplest of signs with the most complex language.

Setting and staging

Jacobean theatres had a large playing space, but the surrounding tiered galleries for the audience created a sense of intimacy (see pages 13–14). The backdrop, with its carved wooden facia enclosing three entrances, the central discovery space and the raised gallery (indicated in stage directions by *above*) were conventional, but could be varied in their use. A curtained discovery space may have been used to show the body of Antonio's wife (I.iv), the Duke and Duchess in bed (II.iii), Junior in prison (III.iv), and the *unsunnèd lodge* (III.v.18). The raised gallery may have supported the musicians at the banquet (V.iii).

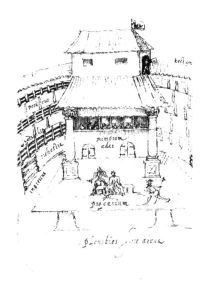

Johannes de Witt's sketch of the Swan Theatre in about 1596

The large central rear entrance may have been used to bring out larger props such as the bier, the royal bed and the banqueting table. Alternatively this entrance could have been adorned with a canopy, offering a visual focus, and used for the formal entrance of the opening procession, as a frame for the judges' bar or the Duke's throne in the trial scene, for a canopied royal bed, or for Junior's prison cell. The movement of the actors was always downstage, from rear to front stage towards the audience, allowing for a close relationship between actor and audience in a soliloquy or aside.

Smaller props were simple; the necessary objects included swords, daggers, torches, prayer books, skulls, severed heads, gold coins, chains and locks, signet rings, and some inscribed parchment. Audiences enjoyed special effects, such as the blazing star in V.iii, which was probably created by using a metal container to burn fats with iron filings and create sparks. Jacobeans were

183

skilled in pyrotechnics and could easily have created an effect that lasted a minute or so.

The 'blocking' of characters – how they are dispersed over the stage – is another important effect. Groups of characters could be arranged in horizontal layers with the more important actions or speeches taking place at the front. Vindice's position would often be at the front edge of the stage, and this would immediately suggest both his significance to the drama and his marginal, edgy relationship with the court. Dialogue could move quickly from group to group on different parts of the stage, at times over-lapping.

Activity

Explore Middleton's stagecraft in I.ii.

Discussion

This complex scene demonstrates Middleton's control of stage space and his skill in directing the attention of his audience. In the original script, where there are no scene divisions, only acts, the introductory stage direction *brought out with Officers for the rape* is important in establishing the first of the four movements that comprise this scene.

At the start, the informality of the preceding family discussion gives way to a more formal scene. The phrase *brought out* indicates that Junior is under guard. Perhaps props were used to present a court setting. A part of the stage would be used as the bar, perhaps the large central entrance. The Duke would probably be seated on a throne, and the judges on chairs. Lesser characters would have benches.

This first part of the scene ends as the stage empties and the Duchess, alone, speaks her soliloquy. Perhaps she moves to the front of the stage and starts speaking even as the other characters are leaving it. Her malice in the soliloquy counterpoints the injustice that has just been witnessed by the audience in the trial, and contrasts with the earlier moments of black humour.

This brief interlude is broken by the entrance of Spurio, who has been the subject of the Duchess's thoughts. The fractious mood is shifted by his pacifying comments to her; this encounter would probably occupy a different stage area. The audience witness a series of character revelations in the exchange between the two, and the outcome is a further two revenge plots.

As the Duchess exits, Spurio takes centre stage, appealing directly to the audience and ratcheting up the tension. The audience become aware of the danger and evil he represents, but also of an interesting conflict of personalities. Each of this unlikely couple is determined to take advantage of the other; who will prove the stronger?

This beautifully orchestrated scene uses the stage space in different ways to draw attention to different perspectives and contrasting moods. The corruption of formal justice in the first part of the scene is widened out and intensified as the audience become aware of corruption in other quarters. Yet the transitions are fluid and naturalistic.

Dramatic structure

The dramatic structure of *The Revenger's Tragedy* is complex. The central scene (III.v) marks the completion of Vindice's first phase of revenge, as Gloriana has been avenged by the Duke's death. Middleton emphasizes that the second phase incorporates the revenger's second function, to purge a corrupt society (III.v.219–220), as well as completing the secondary revenges, such as for Antonio's wife and for the attempt on Castiza's honour.

However, this two-part structure is complicated by a pattern of parallels, where actions after this central point echo earlier ones. For example, the comic interlude where Ambitioso and Supervacuo still think they can plot Junior's release (III.vi.26–28) echoes the Duchess's efforts on his behalf in I.ii; Lussurioso's hiring of Vindice-as-Piato in I.iii is paralleled in his hiring of Vindice the malcontent in IV.ii; and the judgement of the Duchess's sons upon her in IV.iii reflects that of Vindice on his mother (II.i.248–256).

Activity

Analyse the patterns evident in the different scenes of temptation in the play. Discuss the effects achieved.

Discussion

The series of temptations includes a sequence involving the Duchess at I.ii.21–26 and I.ii.118–176, which is paralleled by the actions of her sons in II.iii.67–102. Lussurioso tempts Vindice, beginning at I.iii; Vindice tests his sister and mother in II.i; and Castiza in turn tests Gratiana at IV.iv.99–145.

The Duchess is instrumental in the first two examples, when she pleads with the Duke to avoid punishment for her son, Junior, and then tempts Spurio into taking revenge on the Duke. Similarly Ambitioso and Supervacuo apparently plead for their step-brother's life, but they are consciously being hypocritical as they really wish to see him dead; again, however, it is the Duke's self-interest that dictates his decision rather than the law.

Lussurioso tempts both Vindice and Hippolito when he offers gold and promotion. As in the scenes involving the Duke's corruption of justice, Middleton shows that money and ambition can destroy society.

Vindice's tests of his mother and sister offer a complete contrast; while his mother fails the test, Castiza is resolute. Middleton depicts through Castiza a model of morality and virtue as a touchstone for judgement. The other moral exemplars, Gloriana and Antonio's wife, are both dead. In the second family temptation scene, Gratiana repents and regains her faith, to strengthen this group of virtuous females.

Ironically, the villains have more attractive and striking stage presences, and their arguments in favour of their own wishes and desires are powerful; this is perhaps a comment on the difficulty of achieving virtue in this society and the attractiveness of evil.

Middleton carefully controls the sequencing of events, for example following up a busy public scene (I.ii.1–92) with a dark, personal encounter between two people (I.ii.93–203). The formal, masculine presentation of I.iv is succeeded by a domestic scene foregrounding women in II.i.

In counterpoint to his careful dramatic structuring, the playwright ensures that the events of the plot are driven by accidents and chance rather than successful planning on the part of the characters. For example, it is pure chance that Vindice is hired twice by Lussurioso and once by the Duke; blunders and misunderstandings such as those that lead ultimately to Junior's execution underline the futility of human ambitions. The great comic moments often arise out of farcical situations (see page 161); Middleton seems to ask how human beings can take themselves seriously when they are in control of so little of their lives. Allied to these aspects is the series of delays that hamper many of the revengers' schemes (see pages 168 and 174). The revengers all believe they have autonomy and the ability to pursue their desires, but the audience realize that this is illusory.

Cutting across the linear structure of the plot is the spatial structure of the drama, as revealed by the way the imagery generates meanings that resonate throughout the play. For example, the repeated imagery of poison (see pages 196–197) creates echoes that bring episodes together regardless of time and place. Imagery of time dramatically affects our sense of the pace of the play, as we feel the significance of the *bewitching minute* of pleasure (III.v.74), the *vicious minute* of the rape of Antonio's wife (I.iv.39), and the *false minute* of Spurio's conception (I.ii.167); Vindice's long-awaited vengeance for Gloriana is at last crowded *into a minute* (III.v.122), while society seems to *hurry, hurry, hurry* (II.i.203) towards the devil and damnation. Violent actions occur in a sequence of concentrated moments.

Middleton is precise in his stage directions; they suggest character, as in *the discontented Lord Antonio* (I.iv.1), or setting (III.iv.1), or actions, as in *they all start out of their measure* (V.iii.49), or an effect, as in *A blazing star appeareth* (V.iii.1).

Activity

Analyse the functions of some of the 'asides' in the play.

Discussion

This device is most often used for Vindice. For example, it reveals to the audience Vindice's sheer horror on realizing that his sister is the object of Lussurioso's desires (I.iii.126). In the confrontation between Vindice and his mother, tension is conveyed to the audience through his many asides as Vindice reacts to his mother's weakness, for example at in II.i.105 and 122.

At times the aside is used to create humour, as in Hippolito's mockery of Lussurioso at II.ii.6 and 13–14, and IV.i.5–7, but these asides also have a serious purpose in suggesting the dangerous petulance of the ruler. A similarly comic yet deadly situation is emphasized when Hippolito and Vindice speak aside to discuss how to cope with the tangle they have created through the latter's double disguise (IV.ii.170–174).

Theatricality

Middleton is a self-consciously theatrical writer, as is evident in the dramatic metaphors with which Vindice amuses the audience (see pages 189–190), and when he openly courts approval: *'Twas somewhat witty carried,/ Though we say it* (V.iii.96–97; see also I.i.134 and IV.ii.188–189). Middleton's sense of dramatic timing is superb in the comic episodes in III.vi and V.i.

Middleton also provides spectacle, much loved by the Jacobean audience, as visually arresting scenes merge with the absurd, the grotesque and the lurid. There is the opening procession of extravagantly dressed courtiers; a trial scene; many scenes lit by flickering torchlight (there are multiple references to torches in the play); a Duke and Duchess discovered in bed (II.iii); a Duchess feasting with her secret lover (III.v); a corpse in disguise being stabbed (V.i.71). There are poisoned kisses; death by sword and dagger; grotesque torture scenes; a dumb show followed by a banquet and a blazing star; not one, but two masques; and a final bloody massacre.

Activity

Why does Middleton present the meeting between the Duchess and Spurio onstage in III.v.201–215?

Discussion

Other major events in the plot, such as the murder of Gloriana and the rape of Antonio's wife, occur before the beginning of the action;

Middleton has chosen to present certain dramatic moments. The audience have already seen the Duchess and Spurio together, and their meeting here could have been depicted verbally through a commentary by Vindice. What effects are created by seeing the two characters in this situation?

The first obvious answer is that we witness Vindice torturing the Duke mentally as well as physically in this central scene; Vindice explains to Hippolito that this *most afflicting sight will kill his eyes/ Before we kill the rest of him* (III.v.23–24). The scene alternates moments of black humour and vivid theatricality with incidents of extreme cruelty; the audience, too, are put through extremes of emotion.

Middleton creates effects through imagery. Music, mentioned by Hippolito at the beginning of the sequence and the Duchess at the end, is traditionally an image of harmony, but here suggests the compatibility of two villains who share the same amoral attitude. Likewise, sweetness (201–202) here connotes sinful pleasure.

Shockingly, both the Duchess and Spurio are aware of *sin* (201, 202); both refer to a scheme of divine salvation through *heaven* (204, 206). Picking up the dominant imagery of excess and feasting (215), both turn morality on its head by rejecting virtue in favour of worldly pleasures. Their references to hellfire (207), *poison* (208) and a *sword* (213) make them archetypes of corrupt and violent courtiers. Perhaps this helps prepare the audience to be sympathetic to Vindice as he approaches the second phase of his revenge.

The scene produces a startling visual effect as Middleton presents a tableau of sin. In one area of the stage the audience see the Duke, who is dying physically and spiritually because of his sexual depravity. In another part of the stage the Duchess and Spurio are in a similar state, but do not yet know it. This is a shocking inheritance passed from father to illegitimate son.

Metatheatricality

'Metatheatrical' literally means 'beyond theatre', and refers to those moments when the playwright reminds the audience that they are watching a play. It is often an invitation to consider what they have seen, and to make judgements.

Middleton is audacious not only in the explicit use of theatrical metaphors (see pages 153 and 199) but in reminding his audience of the artificiality of stage conventions such as disguise and the sound of thunder. Sometimes the use of disguise is straightforward for the audience to follow, as when Vindice is disguised as Piato, and sometimes not; is it easy to tell which masquers are which?

Asides (I.iii.144, II.ii.10–11) and references to thunder (IV.ii.201–202, V.iii.42–48) are used by Vindice and Hippolito to emphasize the idea that Lussurioso is a stage villain; the thunder appears to arrive on *cue*. The playwright reminds all present that they are not merely watching an entertainment; they must become active partners with the author, alert to the moral issues that are at stake.

Language and imagery

Variety of language

Thomas Middleton was possibly the most versatile writer in London, creating satiric poems, pamphlets, masques, speeches and plays. Since he was not contracted to any one acting company he could write to a certain extent as he pleased. His drama is rich in range, with satires written for the Children of Paul's, brilliant city comedies and both satiric and high tragedy. This range is also evident in the variety of language he uses in *The Revenger's Tragedy*.

Middleton begins with the conventions of morality drama, evident for example in the allegorical names, such as Vindice, Lussurioso, Ambitioso and Supervacuo; Vindice uses conventionally moralizing language as the play opens: *Duke – royal lecher! Go, gray-haired adultery;/ And thou his son, as impious steeped as he...* But this quickly yields to more naturalistic expression.

Activity

Consider the many references to revenge in the play. What is their effect?

Discussion

References to revenge are frequent but also naturalistic, and the opening scene fulfils many of the expectations of the revenge tragedy audience. Being familiar with the genre, the audience will recognize the introduction of the various motifs associated with it: motive, opportunity, suitable weapons, justification, complicity with a fellow-revenger and the disguise convention are all quickly and plainly established. Vindice speaks of *Vengeance, thou murder's quit-rent* being *tenant to Tragedy* (I.i.39–40) and says that we should *give Revenge her due* (43). Speaking with Hippolito, he anticipates the appearance of *that bald madam, Opportunity* (55) and tells him *Thy wrongs and mine are for one scabbard fit* (57). The scene concludes with Vindice assuming his disguise: *I'll quickly turn into another* (134).

Ideas about revenge are developed through parody in secondary revenge plots, with Spurio also claiming *My revenge is just* (I.ii.190). With references to weapons (*Sword, I durst make a promise of him to thee*, I.iii.171) and to revenge pacts (*I bind you all in steel to bind you surely*, I.iv.57) Middleton builds the language of revenge into a complex interwoven texture.

Vindice intermittently adopts the language of the court to capture precisely that which he condemns: O, *think upon the pleasure of the palace:/ Securèd ease and state* (II.i.196–197). Some readers comment that his use of such language demonstrates that he is contaminated by court society, but that is open to question. His language may simply demonstrate the attractiveness of the sinful option.

The poetry in the set-piece speeches paints vivid pictures of the dark world at the centre of play, steeped in the inverted values of the court. It always furthers the action and our understanding of the characters, as in Vindice's persuasive speech beginning *Who'd sit at home in a neglected room…* (II.i.210), or the Duchess's angry soliloquy *Was't ever known step-duchess was so mild…* (I.ii.93). Spurio's matching soliloquy has an arresting opening line, *Duke, thou didst do me wrong* (I.ii.177), with the hard 'd' sounds expressing his spite and resentment.

As has been noted above, the sharing of lines between characters increases the pace of the dialogue and can have a humorous effect (see pages 163 and 174), but the effect is very different in the first temptation scene between Vindice and Gratiana, when she interrupts his offer of money (*can these persuade you/ To forget heaven*) by quickly accepting it: *Aye, these are they* (II.i.120–121). The language expresses Gratiana's immediate and greedy response, to her son's dismay.

The language often emphasizes speed and recklessness, as in *Now cuckolds are/ A-coining, apace, apace, apace, apace!* (II.ii.143–144); the combination of hard and soft 'c' sounds suggests the brutality and furtiveness of the sexual encounter, while the repetition and punctuation simulate the physical act, and the word *A-coining* links sex to money and power, the prevailing ethos of the court.

Sometimes contrasting meanings are combined in a way that jolts the audience, as when Vindice parodies the tone and conventional attitudes of the court in asking Hippolito whether he is beguiled by the skull: *Here's an eye/ Able to tempt a great man – to serve God* (III.v.54–55). The phrasing reminds the audience of the Duke's rejection of God's laws as he succumbs to the temptations of physical beauty, and that the only thing *great* about him is his lust, while the word *serve* is used for the idea of divine service but also has connotations of animal sex.

Spurio's language can be just as powerful as Vindice's, notably in his soliloquy beginning at I.ii.177, which brings out the similarities between the two characters (see page 172). Spurio and Vindice often echo each other's themes and language, which reinforces the analogy between them. Damning the circumstances of his conception, Spurio speaks of *some stirring dish* at a feast (I.ii.180), while Vindice speaks of *stirring meats* as part of *the pleasure of the palace* (II.i.196–197); Spurio refers to *The sin of feasts, drunken adultery* (I.ii.189), while Vindice speaks of *forgetful feasts,/ And unclean brothels* (III.v.90–91).

The effects in Vindice's powerful lines *Banquets abroad by torchlight, musics, sports…/ Nine coaches waiting – hurry, hurry, hurry!* (II.i.200–203) are created by repetition of 'b' and 's' sounds, by punctuation and by the final triple repetition stressing urgency. Equally powerful effects in Spurio's lines *In such a whisp'ring and withdrawing hour…/ Was I stol'n softly* (I.ii.186–188) are achieved through the sibilant 's' and the breathy 'w' suggesting the secrecy and sensuality of illicit sex. His contemptuous account of drunken *ladies* who *when they rose,/ Were merrily disposed to fall again* (I.ii.182–185) is echoed in Vindice's equally scornful *There's juggling of all sides; some that were maids/ E'en at sunset are now perhaps i' th' toll-book* (II.ii.138–139). In both cases drunkenness, casual sex, the loss of reputation and suggestions of animal sexuality (the *toll-book* is the list of animals for sale at a fair) categorize such women as whores.

Middleton also uses prose to create a range of effects. The opening of the second act, with the entry of Dondolo, who seems incapable of speaking *ordinary words* (II.i.19–20), creates a humorous mood in contrast with the previous scene of men expressing grief and taking solemn oaths (I.iv). In the prose exchanges between Junior and the Keeper and Officers in III.iv, the author suggests that despite their apparent differences in social status, there is little real difference between these men. The colloquial prose dialogue between Vindice and Lussurioso beginning at IV.ii.48 suggests that the situation is certainly not exalted; something is fundamentally wrong, as the jarring prose suggests.

This effect can also be found in some of the verse passages, such as in the overheard liaison between the Duchess and Spurio at III.v.201; like Ambitioso's dialogue with Supervacuo in III.vi, it has a chopped rather than a flowing rhythm and its harshness says much about the moral status of the speakers. Elsewhere, Spurio's extraordinary use of a colloquialism in calling the Duke his *dad* (see page 160) is humorous but underlines the fact that

Spurio's existence is as unfortunate, literally as ill-conceived, as his choice of language.

Rhyming couplets, especially at the ends of scenes, are frequently used for moral sayings or *sententiae*, but these are always appropriate to the character who speaks them. For example, when the Duke says *Age hot is like a monster to be seen:/ My hairs are white, and yet my sins are green* (II.iii.130–131), this is an honest self-judgement revealing internal conflicts about his sinful refusal to adhere to moral law. Sometimes a *sententia* is a platitude or a smug, approving comment. Vindice uses one in *But 'twas decreed before the world began,/ That they should be the hooks to catch at man* (II.i.255–256). The sing-song rhythm, simple rhyme and casual insult to women all point to the cruelty and insincerity of this society. Ambitioso's *sententiae* reveal his vicious but unimaginative nature (III.i.28, III.iii.29–30, III.vi.85–87).

Activity

Analyse the effects of Vindice's meditation on the skull in the central scene of the play (III.v.50–106).

Discussion

These speeches fall into a series of linked points. In lines 50–59, Vindice explains to Hippolito and the audience how the skull can be used as an instrument of temptation or of warning. At lines 60–64 he moves into meditations about female vanity; at 68–70 he is self-critical for assuming the values of the court; at 71–97 he describes that court in terms implying criticism of James I's. Finally, Vindice resumes the mantle of the revenger at lines 98–106. Each part has a slightly different focus and perspective, but the whole builds into an attack on the evils of his society and includes Vindice's self-reproach and his justification for revenge.

The key metaphors used here include:
- the skull as a traditional warning to remember the fact of death (see page 198)
- the image of the *silkworm* (71), suggesting sinful self-indulgence
- the idea of the *bewitching minute* (74) when essential values are sacrificed for momentary gratification.

Vindice's meditations here include direct appeals to the women of the audience (96–97) and to the men (98–100).

Imagery

Middleton's imagery concentrates clusters of meanings and episodes into individual metaphors.

The central concept of transformation is embodied in the image Gratiana uses to describe her return to virtue: *I am recovered of that foul disease* (IV.iv.122). Transformation of a less admirable kind is evident in Vindice's description of *When farmers' sons agreed, and met again/ To wash their hands, and come up gentlemen* (II.i.217–218). In the court of James I many estate owners metaphorically washed their hands of their heritage, abandoning their essential roles on the land in order to seek favour at court. Similarly, the concept of transformation is captured in the equation between gold and justice (as in I.iv.61) and the motif of the power of disguise: *He that did lately in disguise reject thee/ Shall, now thou art thyself, as much respect thee* (IV.ii.3–4). These remarks by Hippolito to his brother are highly ambiguous, raising issues about Vindice's true identity. When is he disguised? Is his disguise literal or metaphorical?

A more sinister image of disguise refers directly to the deceitfulness of society; describing courtiers with their nightly immorality, Vindice asks: *and in the morning,/ When they are up and dressed and their mask on,/ Who can perceive this…?* (I.iii.64–66). This mask conceals the corruption that has taken over society. The mask also smoothes over the loss of self-respect, hence the *forgetful feasts* (III.v.90). Middleton uses images of the skull and the human face to represent the attempt to conceal moral decay, with courtiers in a masque *Putting on better faces than their own* (I.iv.29). The mouth is an opening to hell when men fall for *a delicious lip* (III.v.32).

In contrast, Castiza's claim that *A virgin honour is a crystal tower* (IV.iv.152) expresses the value of consistency and integrity in opposition to the prevailing values. There is the possibility of accepting the divine scheme, a true form of justice that cannot be deceived by masks: *that eternal eye/ That sees through flesh and all* (I.iii.66–67). Similarly, lips need not be suggestive of sin, as *the judge's lips* (III.v.76), should declare true justice.

Middleton's imagery can also be visual, as in the use of medieval emblems in a graphic account of the state of society. Vindice describes such a conceit to Lussurioso: *A usuring father, to be boiling in hell, and his son and heir with a whore dancing over him* (IV.ii.87–89); the usurer, the greedy son and the whore embody the central images of men and women of this society. A similar medieval moral emblem is present when Hippolito stamps on the dying Duke (III.v.155); devils were often depicted stamping on the damned in hell. But what might this suggest about the brothers here?

It is possible to divide the imagery of the play into three clusters (with some inevitable overlaps). The first cluster is that of the symptoms and causes of society's decline. Associated imagery includes that of money (for example, II.i.84–85); of blood in the sense of status (I.iii.101); of clothing (III.v.45); and of jewels (II.i.189), especially the diamond (I.ii.149).

A second group might display the actual processes of change as society heads for hell. This cluster includes images of bloodshed (I.iv.68); of food (I.ii.180); of women (II.i.152–154); of poison (I.iii.167); of decay (II.i.73); of change (III.v.115–116); of the body (I.i.46); and of disease (IV.i.63–64).

The third cluster defines society as being in a state of damnation, being in hell while still on earth (see page 155). This group includes imagery of darkness and disorder (III.v.14); of murder (III.v.219–220); of death (I.ii.13–16); of fire, surely suggestive of hellfire (II.ii.174); and of hell itself (II.ii.22).

Activity

Analyse the ways in which Middleton uses images of poison in *The Revenger's Tragedy*.

Discussion

Imagery of poison, linked to images of disease and of serpents, is important in conveying the author's idea that this society is sickened to the point of death. The *black serpent* mentioned by Castiza is a poisonous snake; it is also an image of the devil (IV.iv.131).

Literal acts of poisoning are used as a base from which to move into other levels of meaning. Before the play begins, the Duke has poisoned Gloriana; Vindice plans to poison the Duke with the same *drug* (III.v.102). In the same scene, the Duchess threatens to poison the (already poisoned) Duke (line 208).

Vindice's words make explicit the links between poison, gold and moral/spiritual death when he reacts to Lussurioso's bribe with the words *I've eaten noble poison* (I.iii.167). However, the concept of poison is mitigated here by the word *noble*; perhaps this unavoidable dose might lead to a good outcome. But can poison ever have beneficial effects? Is Vindice deluding himself?

Castiza expresses the idea that the poisoning of the soul by sin is like being possessed by a devil: *Mother, come from that poisonous woman there!* (II.i.236). Vindice likewise claims that his mother's *breast/ Is turned to quarled poison* (IV.iv.6–7).

Middleton extends the notion of poison to include the corruption of law and justice when Vindice, posing as the malcontent, speaks to Lussurioso about abuse of the system of justice: *There are old men at the present, that are so poisoned with the affectation of law words...* (IV.ii.58–59). This underlines the impact of Junior's abortive trial (I.ii).

Middleton's other significant sequences of imagery, for example that of gold, of jewellery, and of blood, work in a similar way.

The significance of the skull

Middleton presents the skull of Gloriana in three different ways in *The Revenger's Tragedy*:

- as a *memento mori* (I.i.1–90, III.v.50–116)
- as the Jacobean whore (III.v.43–97, 132–145)
- as Gloriana (I.i.14–49, III.v.50–121, 147–199).

The skull as a *memento mori*

Memento mori is a Latin phrase meaning 'Remember you will die'. It is an ancient tradition that one function of art is to remind people of the fact of death, and that they must prepare for it.

The skull appears at the opening of the play in the hands of Vindice as he comments on the parade of depraved characters. It is used to signify the sinfulness and depravity of the court as Vindice addresses it in his account of his fiancée's death:

> Thee when thou wert appareled in thy flesh
> The old duke poisoned,
> Because thy purer part would not consent
> Unto his palsy-lust

(I.i.31–34)

We realize that the characters we have seen passing across the stage are part of a grotesque masque as they are in a sense already dead spiritually and morally. In this case, are we, the audience, watching a parade in hell? Is this court hell itself? Where inside the theatre do its boundaries lie; do they extend off-stage?

Vindice's description of his living fiancée arouses ambivalent responses as his language reveals the attitudes and values of the court. Her eyes are referred to as *diamonds* (I.i.19), establishing the imagery of gold and jewels which becomes a dominant cluster throughout the play (see page 196); similarly he establishes the prevailing misogynistic (anti-female) tone, for the living woman was apparently seen not so much as victim but as tempter (see page 202), able to persuade a man to *Melt all his patrimony in a kiss* (I.i.27). Is Vindice contaminated by these values? Or do his references to heaven, purity and virtue reveal his own goodness? Either way, the skull as an emblem suggests the corruption of the age as well as the imperative to revenge which determines the narrative trajectory of the play. It is likely to remain visible to the audience throughout this scene, perhaps placed by Vindice at the front of the stage.

On its next appearance in III.v, the skull becomes a device for revealing what really lies beneath the mask, the disguise, the painted lip and cheek, the hypocritical pretence and the lies that characterize this society. It shows the inevitable fate of human beings, who can deceive each other *but cannot deceive worms* (III.v.97). Vindice explicitly refers to the skull as a *memento mori* when he says *It were fine, methinks,/ To have thee seen at revels, forgetful feasts,/ And unclean brothels…*(III.v.89–91).

The skull as the Jacobean whore

The skull represents all the betrayed and victimized women of the play and of the court. In the central scene of the play where Vindice uses it to poison the Duke, it becomes the *concubine* (III.v.42) procured to satisfy the Duke's lust. The skull is formally introduced, in a wonderful piece of theatre, as a dramatic character, another instance of transformation in the play. The stage directions at line 42 make it plain that the skull is elaborately disguised; the reference to masquers' attire links it to the imagery of clothing and disguise throughout the play. The exposed skull of a pure woman seen in the opening scene of the play has been transformed shockingly into the representative woman of the court, the Jacobean whore. Emblematically it represents both the virgin (as Vindice's virtuous fiancée) and the whore, the two poles of female existence in *The Revenger's Tragedy* (see pages 201–204).

References to the theatre and its conventions emphasize the symbolism of Vindice's actions. He draws attention to the stage setting as *this luxurious circle* (22), speaks of a *useless property* (100), and comments that *When the bad bleeds, then is the tragedy good* (199). The language and setting also emphasize sinfulness in this scene, with its *darkened, blushless angle* (14). In *this unsunnèd lodge* (18), God's natural sunlight cannot penetrate – it is the devil's domain. Natural disorder suggests moral disorder, as *'tis night at noon* (19).

Vindice offers a grotesque parody of a *proud and self-affecting dame* (83) preparing for revelry at her dressing table. In a mood of black farce, he uses the skull to act out an encounter between a living woman and the Duke's bawd as he prepares her for the assignation to come. He assures her that it will remain secret, that she will be richly rewarded for prostituting herself, and that this is the best thing she could do to advance herself socially (43–47). This is an ironic summary of the arguments with which Vindice tested Castiza and her mother in II.i. Simultaneously, Vindice is performing the same task for Gloriana's skull as he physically prepares it for the fatal encounter with her killer.

The skull as Gloriana

When Vindice reveals that the name of his *betrothèd lady* (I.i.16) was *Gloriana* (III.v.150), Middleton's audience would recognize the significance of this reference: it is one of the poetic names Edmund Spenser uses for Elizabeth I in his epic poem *The Faerie Queene* (1590–1596). This is an allegorical romance in which knights fight to preserve honour and virtue; it was written in praise of the queen. The name *Gloriana* reminds the audience of the better days of the old queen's reign compared to the corruption and extravagance that James I brought to the English throne in 1603.

In *The Faerie Queene* there are three manifestations of the Tudor queen: Mercilla, Gloriana, and Belphoebe. As Mercilla in Book V, Elizabeth is represented as a famous 'mayden queene'; as Gloriana, she represents justice and tradition as Spenser offers a list of her historical forebears (Book II); as Belphoebe (Book IV), she represents chastity defeating the evil 'Salvage Man', who allegorically represents Lust. Middleton presents the skull of Gloriana in parallel ways in *The Revenger's Tragedy*. Vindice emphasizes her purity and virginity (like Mercilla); the skull defeats the Duke's lust with a kiss (like Belphoebe); the skull will also become the instrument for justice in the punishment of the Duke (like Spenser's Gloriana).

There are other possible borrowings from Spenser's poem. Sir Guyon (or Sir Gawain) represents restraint or temperance as he destroys Acrasia's seductive Bowre of Blisse (Book II); perhaps

Middleton echoes this in the figure of Vindice, who is celibate, appalled at the lust of the court, and has waited patiently for the appropriate moment to act. He is the avenger of outraged chastity on behalf of Gloriana, Castiza and Antonio's wife. In killing the Duke, who represents Lust, in the *unsunnèd lodge* where he intends to meet *a lady* (III.v.18, 12), Vindice similarly destroys a 'Bowre of Blisse'.

Themes of the play

Women

In seventeenth-century London, women were debarred from full citizenship and led generally restricted lives. A wealthy married woman, however, ran a complex household; as a widow, she could take over her husband's trade; a single woman could enter a trade in partnership with a brother. A poorer woman might become a housemaid, or be bound into one of the lower-paid apprenticeships rejected by men, such as the manufacture of gloves or lace. A very poor woman might be forced into prostitution.

Middleton presents five female characters in *The Revenger's Tragedy*, three living (the Duchess, Gratiana and Castiza) and two dead, with Gloriana present as a skull, and the nameless Antonio's wife seen as a corpse. Yet dead or alive, these women are all subject to men who contest ownership and control of them, whether by temptation (Gratiana), seduction (Castiza), marriage and adultery (the Duchess), or as motives for revenge, as is the case for Gloriana and Antonio's wife. There is no escape from male tyranny.

The patriarchal nature of Jacobean society, as reflected in *The Revenger's Tragedy*, is immediately made apparent in the protagonist Vindice's dismissive attitude towards women (*Wives are but made to go to bed and feed*, I.i.132) and his obsession with their virginity and chastity. The honour code is that of the traditional masculine, aristocratic system which is fixated on attempting to control female sexuality.

Lussurioso's designs on Castiza therefore attack the very root of Vindice's social status, which he had assumed he could protect from the corruption of the court. When Antonio's wife commits suicide after the loss of her chastity to rape, Antonio describes her body to the assembled nobles as *a fair, comely building newly fall'n,/ Being falsely undermined* (I.iv.2–3). He perceives her as a commodity, equating the woman's body to a valuable piece of property. His wife aligned herself with this patriarchal philosophy by committing suicide, choosing death rather than the shame that would have been heaped upon her as a survivor of rape. Her concern for chastity is emphasized in the symbols she selects at her death, the prayer-books and the reading 'It is better to die in virtue than to live in disgrace' (I.iv.17). The chastity of their female relatives secures for Vindice and Antonio an older, more noble and aristocratic code of honour, which the court has rejected by its deeds, if not its words.

While women are most desirable as properties, they are also a potent threat. The reverse side of the obsession with chastity is the mistrust with which women are viewed; they are regarded as tempters who draw men towards evil, *the hooks to catch at man* (II.i.256). Spurio notes that *one incestuous kiss picks open hell* (I.ii.174). As we have seen (page 199), when Gloriana's skull is *dressed up in tires* (III.v.42) and anointed with poison, it becomes an emblem of the conventional medieval opposition between virgin and whore; in a man's hands, a woman's body becomes a means of tempting and punishing sinners, an object and an instrument.

Female anatomy is seen as both vulnerable and dangerous. Vindice comments: *That woman is all male, whom none can enter* (II.i.112); the degrading verb *enter* again turns the woman into a property, like a castle, whose gates are guarded by certain men and attacked by others. Middleton creates an ironic parallel to Vindice's use of this verb when Lussurioso tempts Vindice and gives him money, saying *And thus I enter thee*. Vindice responds: *This Indian devil/ Will quickly enter any man* (I.iii.86–87). Gold, the devil and a woman's body are drawn together by this imagery, and the implication is clear: women and money are the routes to damnation.

Vindice makes this male viewpoint explicit: *Were't not for gold and women, there would be no damnation* (II.i.253).

Women are valued for their beauty, yet blamed for being preoccupied with their appearance. Religion is invoked to support this view; Vindice scorns the vain woman who will *grieve her Maker* with her concern for *her superfluous outside* (III.v.84–86).

Activity

What functions are served by the character of the Duchess?

Discussion

The Duchess is defined (as is appropriate for a woman in this society) by her attitude towards her husband (I.ii.93–108, III.v.205–208) and her sons (I.ii.21–26, 102–105). She is clearly intelligent, as can be seen in her manipulation of Spurio (I.ii.145–154), although she is amoral (I.ii.155–157; III.v.202; IV.iii.3–4). She performs an essential role in the development of the revenge drama, triggering responses from Spurio (I.ii, III.v), her own sons (IV.iii), and Lussurioso (V.iii.7). She seems to energize the evil-doers.

Her language makes many references to heaven, hell and damnation (see the Activity on page 188). Although she seems aware of her moral and spiritual duties and of the Christian scheme of salvation and damnation, pointing up these issues for the audience, she focuses on immediate gratification and the pursuit of revenge.

In such a society a woman could only perform certain roles, and motherhood was the virtuous ideal for the married woman. Her duty was to support the patriarchy by producing male heirs. But women have intelligence and free will, and the Duchess uses her prerogative over her own body in embarking upon an affair with Spurio. Middleton makes it clear that her action is one of revenge against her husband: *I'll kill him in his forehead.../ That wound is deepest* (I.ii.107–108). The clever, ruthless woman causes havoc to patriarchal social codes, and by taking on a masculine role in seducing Spurio she plays the men at their own game.

Middleton's female characters are central to the retributive pattern of the play, both as victims and as threats. They have a certain degree of autonomy and most are confronted with moral choices. Castiza is strong in defence of her chastity, even though this condemns her to social isolation and poverty; Gratiana initially bends to the male will in agreeing to tempt her daughter, but eventually chooses grace. Gloriana's skull and Antonio's wife's body remind the audience of the violations they have suffered. It could be argued that Vindice enables Gloriana to gain her own revenge from beyond the grave. However, it is perhaps the amoral Duchess who, by taking on masculine roles as seducer and revenger, most effectively challenges the prevailing ethos and reveals its essential vulnerability.

The abuse of power

The Revenger's Tragedy considers issues raised by the despotic power of ruling tyrants, and the effects of this power on the individual subject, his or her aspirations, and family life. This is often interpreted as veiled criticism of the court of James I.

Vindice has every reason to be outraged by the Duke's poisoning of Gloriana, and later by Lussurioso's plot to seduce Castiza. In this society Vindice has certain rights and responsibilities as head of his household; it is his duty to protect the honour of his family in name and person. The Duke's murder of Gloriana and his son's intended corruption of Castiza are symptomatic of a diseased society, which is poisoned from its ruler downwards. There is no sense of individual rights, or of traditional order being respected: despotic and corrupt rulers deny all that is due to the nobility, gentry and lower orders of society. Vindice seems perfectly right to feel outrage against and try to overthrow such rulers.

The Duke denies any concept of justice (see page 209). But he does not simply deny human rights, he denies the rights of God himself. He perverts the idea of sin (*Give me that sin that's robed in holiness*, III.v.140) as well as punishment. His son Lussurioso acts similarly. Lussurioso is wholly aware of the power he has over unfortunate subjects: *There's hope in him, for discontent and want/ Is the best clay to mould a villain of* (IV.i.47–48).

The metaphor of shaping a man from clay is borrowed from biblical accounts of God's creation of humankind, and reveals the dangerous illusions of the tyrant. He is aware that his people live in a state of subjection, but in enlisting Vindice he seeks to demean his status further to that of *villain*.

The danger of being in Lussurioso's service is made explicit: *He that knows great men's secrets and proves slight,/ That man ne'er lives to see his beard turn white* (IV.i.66–67). This is uttered as a *sententia* (see page 194) and the rhyme chillingly underlines his utter lack of concern. This is reinforced in the next scene with the arrogant aside *Deep policy in us makes fools of such:/ Then must a slave die when he knows too much* (IV.ii.195–196). The noun *slave* and the imperative verb *must die* indicate his contempt for his subjects and the shocking rights of life and death that such tyrants take upon themselves. The power of life and death should belong to a properly constituted court of law under a just ruler, and ultimately to God.

On succeeding to the ducal throne, Lussurioso's judgements even on his own family are harsh. After banishing the Duchess (V.iii.7), he plans the deaths of his half-brother and step-brothers:

The bastard shall not live. After these revels,
I'll begin strange ones; he and the stepsons
Shall pay their lives for the first subsidies.

(V.iii.8–10)

The horrific metaphor of *strange* court revels suggests that matters of life and death are only a game or an entertainment to him.

In an ironical parallel, the fear of violent challenge to his rule is the reason that Antonio will use for the sentence passed on the two revengers: *You that would murder him would murder me* (V.iii.104). Will the new ruler be any more protective of individual rights? It seems rather doubtful.

In his plot against Lussurioso, Vindice attempts to lead a rebellion against *those few nobles that have long suppressed you* (V.ii.11). He persuades these lords that they can purge the obvious corruption, and urges them to:

> Strike old griefs into other countries
> That flow in too much milk and have faint livers,
> Not daring to stab home their discontents.
>
> (V.ii.2–4)

Is this a hint to Middleton's English audience to think about their own country, where a spirit of rebellion against the excesses of James I's rule might be justified?

Although his plots against the Duke and Lussurioso succeed, Vindice exemplifies the fate of the individual in this society. His comment *I'm hired to kill myself* (IV.ii.207) draws attention to a farcical and absurd notion, yet this suggests a tragic path for the protagonist, as perhaps assuming the role of Piato turns the just revenger into a cold and calculating assassin. Perhaps Middleton is suggesting that the veneer of civilization is frighteningly thin, and that evil lies not far below the surface in everyone. This is an extreme Calvinist notion (see page 178) that offers a bleak vision of society. On the other hand, perhaps Middleton is simply presenting the consequences of a lack of hope for a decent way of life in a society as fundamentally corrupt as this.

In the world of the play there is no confirmation of a divine scheme of salvation; the universe seems indifferent to the suffering of humankind, and divine intervention seems to be absent or, at best, arbitrary. To most of Middleton's audience, to live without the certainty of a Christian scheme of salvation would mean living without any moral framework, so there could be no grasp of 'sin' or 'grace' and no justice.

However, although Gratiana is tempted, she repents, and Castiza only pretends to yield to corrupt persuasion in order to test her mother. What virtue there is in the play is embedded in family life, although these people are both isolated and powerless.

The court of James I

Middleton takes risks in presenting veiled criticism of the court of James I. This criticism can be seen, for example, in Vindice's comments on the destruction caused to traditional social structures as the landed gentry flock to court to seek patronage, leaving *patrimonies washed a-pieces* (I.iii.51) and resulting in lands being sold to finance fine clothing. Court favourites are *Swelled up with jewels* (I.ii.112), and when Lussurioso assumes power he immediately demonstrates the way that the most abject flattery is rewarded (V.iii.29–36). The purpose of court life seems to be to indulge in pleasures such as a *gluttonous dinner* and *impudent wine and lust* (I.ii.180, 191).

While the Duke and his courtiers live for pleasure, they deny the rights of their subjects and even threaten their lives. Subjects seem to have three options: they can live in poverty like Gratiana and Castiza (II.i.1–8); they can risk their own and their family's wellbeing as Vindice's father did in attempting to find favour at court (I.i.126–127, III.v.167–169); or they can compromise their principles, sacrifice their rights and endanger their lives in the corrupt service of a tyrannical ruler.

James I presided over a court that was criticized for extravagance and favouritism

Criticism of the court of James I can be inferred from recurring motifs in the play. One of the most prominent motifs is that of sinful excess, seen in the many references to food and feasting, and the sexual sins that are associated with this. Other motifs include extravagance and favouritism, the abuse of justice, the denial of the autonomy of the individual subject, the suppression of women by the social code, and the destruction of the safeguards provided by the feudal aristocratic system.

Activity

Explore the ways in which Middleton presents the motif of sinful excess in *The Revenger's Tragedy*.

Discussion

Vindice and Spurio, as we have already seen, are central in presenting the attractiveness of vice and sin, and an analysis of Vindice's speech to Hippolito at II.ii.134–146 reveals some of Middleton's methods. The use of imagery, register, and poetic and rhetorical devices creates powerful effects.

- Imagery: The opening image of the setting for a night's debauchery, linking it to a *funeral* (lines 134–136), suggests social disarray. The metaphor of a *full sea* (137) suggests a society immersed in sin. The image of *cuckolds* that are *A-coining* (143–144) links sexual activity to the money motif that is so dominant in this play, while the reference to the *sisters* who *spin* (145) subverts the classical image of the Fates who spin the threads of people's individual destinies, to suggest the helplessness of the individual in the face of temptations in such a corrupt court.

- Register: There are repeated references to illicit sexual behaviour (such as *juggling*, line 138) and adjectives that suggest sinfulness, such as the *immodest* clothing in line 140. The reference to a lover arriving *by water* (141) suggests a scene on the banks of the River Thames, placing these activities squarely in Middleton's London.

- Poetic and rhetorical devices: The opening apostrophe to *Night* immediately establishes the link between physical and moral darkness, and between night-time and sin. Middleton uses enjambment to suggest the ease with which one act leads to another (for example, at lines 134–136). The multiple repetition of *apace, apace, apace, apace!* (144) almost hypnotizes the listeners onstage and in the audience into complicity, while the alliteration of the 's' sound establishes the soft seductiveness of sin.

Elsewhere, Vindice's words to his mother at II.i.196–229 and Spurio's powerful account of the circumstances of his conception at I.ii.179–189 work in similar ways. Middleton wants his audience to feel the attractiveness of the luxurious lifestyle in order to understand how easy it is to yield to temptation.

Justice

The issue of justice is a prominent theme in *The Revenger's Tragedy*. The play offers suggestions of a divine frame of law and justice (although it is chiefly notable for its remoteness from this society) through references to God, heaven, angels, grace and virtue, all traditional Christian terms. Running parallel to this is a concern for the lack of secular justice. According to Christian beliefs, human judgements should be made in the light of divine guidance, but while the privileged characters pay lip service to their God and to religious belief, they seem to act purely out of short-term self-interest.

A surprising number of scenes are centred on the pursuit of justice under the law, including Junior's trial (I.ii), the Duke's considerations of justice over the apparent treason of Lussurioso (II.iii), and Ambitioso's and Supervacuo's schemes to avoid justice for Junior while promoting the harshest punishment for Lussurioso. The issue is developed further in Junior's scene with his Keeper and the Officers (III.iv). Ironically, justice can be seen to be served when Junior is 'mistakenly' executed at the end of this scene. This is immediately followed by the central scene of the play, in which the driving force behind Vindice and Hippolito's actions is their thirst for justice, which they pursue through even more unorthodox methods. The grotesque cruelty inflicted on the Duke is as far as can be imagined from notions of the purity and objectivity of justice.

Yet Vindice often uses terms that suggest the presence of an eternal and divine frame of justice. He speaks of *that eternal eye/ That sees through flesh and all* (I.iii.66–67); he calls on angels to protect and celebrate his sister's virtue (II.i.137, 241); and he twice calls out for divine retribution (II.i.250–252, IV.ii.197–202). Castiza reminds her mother of the existence of damnation (II.i.204), and Gratiana, as has been discussed, exemplifies the redemption of a sinner though grace (see page 180). On his succession, Antonio acknowledges the law of God: *Just is the law is above* (V.iii.90; see also line 128, the final line of the play).

This acknowledgement of a higher divine power is not confined to the 'virtuous' characters, as Lussurioso speaks of human readiness *to err*, even in the face of *hell* (I.iii.73). But he does not seem to apply any such standards to himself, and directly challenges what could be an omen of judgement on him personally, in the form of a comet (V.iii.18–21). The Duchess, too, acknowledges in a general way that eternal damnation is the judgement on sinners, when she speaks of *the justice/ Of that unbribèd, everlasting law* (I.ii.162–163). Perhaps the audience will remember this comment when her two sons bribe the gaolers in III.iii.24–25.

Spurio shows more concern about the morality of his own actions as he wonders about sin (III.v.201) and claims that his *revenge is just* (I.ii.190). It is Vindice, of course, who is most concerned with the ethics of revenge, telling the tormented Duke that *heaven is just* (III.v.182). But there is an irony here, since the code of the revenger is not that of divine law (see page 167).

As for the concept of civil justice within society, the trial of Junior presents the shocking and outright corruption of justice for which the Duke is responsible. Initially he pays lip service to the concept of justice and claims that Junior's crime must be punished to avoid *shame* (I.ii.10) being heaped on his court. The First Judge upholds this view, as to act otherwise would bring judgement itself into disrepute (I.ii.58–59), and he pleads for the acceptance of the legal sentence, *'Tis but the justice of the law* (I.ii.71). However, the Duchess's intervention succeeds and the Duke prefers to avoid the issue and *defer the judgement* (I.ii.83).

In the case of Lussurioso's potentially treasonous act, the Duke again consults his own convenience rather than the law. In an important soliloquy, the Duke makes the grave admission implied in the comment that *It well becomes that judge to nod at crimes/ That does commit greater himself, and lives* (II.iii.123–124). Justice is explicitly subordinated to self-interest, as is frankly advocated by the Duchess, who thinks that the Duke should allow her son to *walk/ With a bold foot upon the thorny law,/ Whose prickles should bow under him* (I.ii.103–105).

Spurio recognizes how the law is treated at court: *flattery and bribes will kill it* (I.ii.90). These are the words of an informed insider. The murder of Gloriana, the rape of Antonio's wife and the threat to Castiza speak of the effects of such corruption. However, at least there has been a trial in the case of the rape; in the summary judgements made later in the play, there will be no such opportunity for justice.

The three concepts of justice – the divine frame, the revenger's personal and public task, and the tyranny of state injustice – are brought neatly together in Vindice's stirring call to rebellion:

> Let our hid flames break out, as fire, as lightning,
> To blast this villainous dukedom vexed with sin;
> Wind up your souls to their full height again.

> (V.ii.5–7)

All three elements are in place, with the references to a divine frame in the words *sin* and *souls*, to the personal and public revenge on Lussurioso's *villainous dukedom*, and to the determination to achieve state justice, which has been seen to overpower individual morality and suppress the courtiers' spiritual *height*. The reference to *lightning* suggests that this course of action is natural and therefore health-giving; the mention of *fire* suggests the fate of Lussurioso, who is surely bound for hell. The *flames* are not simply those of rebellion, but might be the flames of wisdom representing the Holy Spirit. Vindice still seems certain of divine approval for his actions; is the audience?

Activity

The rulers make several summary judgements in the final act of *The Revenger's Tragedy*. What is the effect of these examples of state justice?

Discussion

In the last act of the play, three such judgements are made; the first is by Lussurioso on the innocent First Gentleman, who had merely conveyed the Duke's message to the court: *Bear him straight/ To execution* (V.i.137–138). It is a summary decision in which the victim has no chance of establishing his innocence. Shockingly Antonio, the hoped-for saviour of the state, behaves in exactly the same way not once, but twice. In the first instance, the Fourth Man is wrongly sentenced for Lussurioso's death: *Let him have bitter execution* (V.iii.72). Yet there is irony here, as this man did in fact kill Spurio, so perhaps a measure of justice has been achieved without human agency. Then Antonio is equally peremptory in his sentencing of Vindice and Hippolito: *Bear 'em to speedy execution* (V.iii.101). His use of the word *speedy* is an uncomfortable echo of Lussurioso's *straight.*

It is a pessimistic conclusion, as it seems that while divine justice is unavailable, state justice is an illusion. While the Duke and Lussurioso both corrupt the course of justice, Antonio simply ignores its claims.

Issues raised by the play's title

Why is the word *Revenger's* of the title in the singular? Why isn't it *The Revengers' Tragedy*, when there are so many revengers in the play? And is the play a tragedy?

Vindice is clearly the primary revenger and the protagonist of the play; he is immediately identified by his allegorical name, which suggests 'Vengeance', and by his mention of revenge in his opening commentary: *Vengeance, thou murder's quit-rent...* (I.i.39). In terms of the revenge genre convention, he has justified motives against the Duke for poisoning his fiancée, and against Lussurioso for threatening his sister's chastity. In strict accordance with the genre, as we have seen, he also undertakes the second part of the revenger's role, to purge the corrupted state. Vindice makes this clear to Antonio: *Your hair will make the silver age again* (V.iii.85). Furthermore, he has the sympathy of the audience (see pages 163–164); he appeals to them by his courage, dedication to his task, black humour and the apparent openness of the comments he directs to them.

Hippolito too is a justified revenger, as he binds the lords on his sword to revenge Antonio's wife (I.iv.57), but he is clearly secondary to his older sibling, although he is quick-witted and at times initiates their schemes (as at I.i.58). He is the primary revenger's willing accomplice and assistant as he begs his older brother to let him in on his scheme: *You vowed once/ To give me share to every tragic thought* (III.v.5–6).

Of the other revengers in the play, the Duchess, Spurio and Lussurioso are motivated by malice and their actions are rooted in evil, so none of them can achieve tragic status. Ambitioso and Supervacuo are slightly different as they are foolish as well as malicious. They are also ready to plot against each other even while they are apparently in league against their rivals, and are willing to kill each other to secure power. This is the biblical sin of Cain against Abel; brother kills brother.

As for the word *Tragedy* in the title, can Vindice's life and death be termed a tragedy? It's a complex question, but his circumstances certainly are tragic. In terms of the revenge genre, he has a most unfortunate role. (The place of Vindice in the revenge tragedy genre is discussed in the Activity on page 167.) Revenge is thrust upon him by the unjust actions of the Duke and his son; his task is justified in both its private and public aspects, and he believes that God can see through to his heart and witness the purity of his intentions with *that eternal eye/ That sees through flesh and all* (I.iii.66–67). It is a particularly appropriate image as Vindice is metaphorically wearing a mask as he speaks, in the form of his disguise as Piato, *that knave* (I.i.93).

However, while revenge is potentially acceptable to a Jacobean audience it remains a sin in the eyes of God and a crime against the state. The role of the revenger is an isolated and thankless one; he is destined to die a martyr. In terms of Vindice's social role, too, desperate circumstances have been forced upon him; his poverty compels him into service, where he is made to *forget my nature* (I.iii.180). His employer Lussurioso is often linked with the devil. When he says, on first hearing of Vindice, *There's hope in him, for discontent and want/ Is the best clay to mould a villain of* (IV.i.47–48), the Christian virtue of *hope* is degraded to evil purposes and, as we have seen, he is characterizing himself as a creator of villains, in a parody of God's divine act of creation. By placing Vindice in such demonic circumstances, Middleton is emphasizing the tragic aspects of his situation.

At the end of the play, as befits a tragic hero, Vindice accepts his fate; he has fulfilled his obligations. In an understated way, he faces death with courage and even humour.

Activity

Consider the significance of the short scene V.ii in preparing for the end of the play.

Discussion

This brief scene is unusual as we see Vindice in a totally different context; he is the rebel leader inspiring loyalty among his peers. The audience realize that grievances against the ducal family are widespread, and that Vindice is far from alone in his desire for justice.

With this scene, does Middleton extend his presentation of Vindice, to emphasize that he is a just revenger who is forced into ridding the state of a corrupt dynasty for the good of others as well as himself? Does the revenger even sacrifice himself in the pattern of Jesus Christ's sacrifice on the cross to redeem humankind?

The language used suggests the appropriateness of Vindice's action, which aims *To blast this villainous dukedom vexed with sin* (V.ii.6). His second, public revenge seems to be as just as his first, personal vengeance. Vindice's language also suggests the purity of his motives as he calls upon his fellow-conspirators to *Let our hid flames break out, as fire, as lightning* (line 5). The reference to *lightning* suggests the means that God might use to intervene, and therefore divine approval. References to nature also suggests the appropriateness of the planned murder. Perhaps the terms *flames* and *fire* foreshadow the appearance of the *blazing star* in the next scene, proof that there is a supernatural framework far more powerful than the ducal family.

Yet Middleton is again ambiguous, as these references could also suggest the *flames* of hell. Is that where Vindice's mission will take him? In contrast to earlier in the play, for example in his reference to the *eternal eye* at I.iii.66, Vindice makes no direct reference to God or divine justice here, although such references are implied.

Middleton's purposes are complex in this vital short scene, and it is crucial in determining audience response to Vindice in the action-packed scene that follows it and concludes the play. In the final scene, the revenger does make references to divine law and justice: *When thunder claps, heaven likes the tragedy* (V.iii.48). His last lines are important in determining our response to him:

> but we hate
> To bleed so cowardly. We have enough,
> I' faith, we're well: our mother turned, our sister true,
> We die after a nest of dukes – adieu.

> (V.iii.122–125)

The register here is obliquely Christian; his sacrifice for society is stressed in his willingness to *bleed* for humanity, perhaps an echo of Christ's sacrifice. At his death, Vindice's rejoicing focuses on his mother's restoration to Christian virtue and his sister's strong beliefs. He could also be asserting his own belief with the oath *I'faith*. The last line is complex. The phrase *nest of dukes* reminds the audience of a nest of snakes, as this is a common collective noun for such a colony; this in turn recalls the imagery of poison and serpents in the play (see pages 196–197), bringing the devil to mind. Has Vindice banished the devil from his society? Within six years, John Webster would echo this phrase in his play *The White Devil:* 'The bed of snakes is broke' (V.iii.255).

Vindice's last word is *adieu,* which is not a secular farewell; its literal meaning is 'to God'. Is he commending the audience and himself to the judgement, and hopefully care, of God?

The Revenger's Tragedy in performance

The Revenger's Tragedy was probably first performed in 1606 by the King's Men at the outdoor Globe Theatre. R.V. Holdsworth suggests that because of 'its northeast orientation' and its large canopy, 'sometimes called "the shadow"', there would have been considerable shade, so torchlight scenes would have made an impression (*Three Jacobean Revenge Tragedies*, see Further Reading page 232). When the *blazing star* appears near the end of the play it would have been dusk, so this special effect would have been striking. Middleton's point that the majestic and awe-inspiring heavenly light created by God overwhelms the puny and sinful torchlight of humankind would have been made very plainly.

Today, *The Revenger's Tragedy* is once again a popular choice among theatre companies because audiences find it fascinating, shocking and exciting. However, modern directors face certain difficulties with the play, such as the use of the disguise convention, so there are often textual changes and cuts. Each director will offer an interpretation that speaks to a particular audience; when you see a play, just as when you read a critical book, it is important to remember that there are always other perspectives to be considered.

Like any great and enduring play, it gives free reign to a director's imagination. An elaborate setting can invoke the opulence of the court, yet sparer sets can also be highly effective. Hippolito describes the court as decked out in *silk and silver* (I.i.52), so a production could feature this central colour scheme and texture. The setting could be altered to suggest any repressive regime – past or present, east or west – as the play's themes are universal; the relationship between power, wealth, politics and sexuality is as current an issue today as when the play was written.

Mentioned even in the opening stage directions, *torchlight* is a dominant motif, and this offers the opportunity for interesting lighting effects. The emblematic skull also presents options for techniques such as laser projection. Visual effects could be enhanced by imaginative use of audio, such as amplified

216

heartbeats to indicate fear or passion, or a musical soundtrack to complement or counterpoint what is being presented onstage.

Of course, a director is free to make the central issues of the play more explicit. For example, the deprivation outside the court could be suggested by the use of tableaux or silent characters, and Gratiana's and Castiza's poverty could be emphasized through contrasts with the court in terms of costume, hair and make-up. There are wonderful possibilities in making more explicit and more central to Lussurioso's character the ideas suggested by Vindice's aside describing him as *a pretty perfumed villain* (I.iii.144). He could be portrayed as bisexual or transvestite, creating the opportunity for some camp humour, but also raising the serious thematic concern about loss of personal identity through depravity in the rich, and oppression in the case of the poor. Similarly the farce and black humour created by the idiocy of the Duchess's sons could be emphasized, but again there is a serious suggestion that their weaknesses are caused by the self-indulgence and materialism of their upbringing, and may even result from generations of in-breeding among aristocrats in a closed society.

Activity

In order to understand the motivations of a character they are to portray, actors often begin with a series of improvisations to establish familiarity with their circumstances and characteristics. Carry out a brief exercise in improvisation based on a scene at Vindice's household after his father dies, his death hastened by *discontent* at the Duke's failure to favour him (as revealed early in the play, I.i.126–127).

Discussion

The four characters involved are his wife Gratiana and daughter Castiza, Vindice the elder son and Hippolito the younger. Remember that Gratiana knows little of her husband's daily life (I.i.130). Using your knowledge of the play, improvise the conversation they might have as they make desperate plans to safeguard their future, since they have been left in financial difficulties. Each character would take a different view.

Notable productions

With the popularization of satire through television and radio programmes, and the success of contemporary black comedy in the theatre, such as Joe Orton's *Loot* in the 1960s, Middleton's plays have become fashionable again. The variety of readings of Vindice used by directors suggests the ambiguity, theatricality and universality of Middleton's protagonist. Many different settings have been used; as well as replicating the original Jacobean setting, directors have chosen to depict Mafia-style societies and post-apocalyptic ones torn apart by class warfare, and stagings have varied from 'punk' style to Art Deco.

1965   The Pitlochry Festival production was directed by Brian Shelton and was played uncut on an Elizabethan-style stage. Vindice stepped into the audience, effectively creating immediacy.

1966   The Royal Shakespeare Company, directed by Trevor Nunn, created a highly successful production that transferred to the Aldwych Theatre. Black and silver were the key colours of the design, which suggested wholesale social and corporate corruption. The link between sex and violence was made explicit. The skull was draped in a black cloak and the Duke began his sexual encounter with it lying on a tombstone. Ian Richardson made a terrifying and witty Vindice, while Alan Howard, playing a bisexual Lussurioso, suggested how this undermined his authority, or gave it a more unpredictable and chilling edge.

1974   The Abbey Theatre, New York presented an abstract character, Vengeance, who supervised the action of the play.

1978   At the Oxford Playhouse, the last scene was made more startling and possibly more pessimistic as the corpses of the Duke and Duchess stood alongside Antonio.

1980   At the Liverpool Playhouse, Peter Lichtenfels' production was true to the original, combining morality elements with horror and black humour to emphasize the ironic reversals, and using a combination of psychological revelation and satire. The set played with scale as huge props dwarfed the players, suggesting human insignificance in the universe.

1985 The production at Magdalen College, Oxford, again suggested that at the end of the play a new form of corrupt government had replaced the old.

1986 Charlotte Bogarde at Manchester University Union directed the play on a tiny stage that created intimacy between players and audience, and was illuminated by powerful strobe lighting. The identical black-masked outfits of the two sets of revengers in the last scene emphasized both the idea of widespread evil and of satire. Lussurioso was played as an immature bully and sex addict; Vindice, on meeting him, took over from his masseur and suggestively tumbled on the floor with him.

1987 Di Trevis directed at the Royal Shakespeare Company to bring out the social perspective, as shadowy figures of beggars flitted periodically across the stage. Elaborate lighting effects and dry ice dramatized the performances, while the opening scene had actors dancing the highly stylized, stately court dance the *pavane*, suggesting rigid social etiquette and also hypocrisy. Antony Sher played Vindice sympathetically as psychologically damaged by his experiences, so the action of the play was, for him, redemptive. On a revolving stage, to the sound of loud dance music, the rape of Antonio's wife was presented while Lussurioso was depicted indulging in fellatio behind a wall. The dark energy of the court and of the Jacobean world was evident. Archive video of this production is available at the Shakespeare Centre Library and Archive (see Further Reading page 234).

2000 At Cornell University, New York, Margaret Collins and Jeremy Lopez cast a female Vindice, perhaps suggesting the universality of the play. The set represented various types of decline with a diagonal ramp running across the stage from the upper right. Set alongside this were triple mirrors, highly effective in Vindice's role playing, which allowed the audience to see themselves and seemed to urge them to make judgements. Music ranged from classical to contemporary. Supertramp's 'Breakfast in America', with its lyric 'Take a look at my girlfriend, she's the only one I got', ironically introduced Castiza. That song may have been even more effective as Vindice introduced the skull to Hippolito and the audience.

2002 Alex Cox directed a film version, available on DVD (see Further Reading page 234), with a starry cast. Christopher Ecclestone makes an overwhelmingly powerful Vindice (see photo on page 155), yet Cox creates sympathy for him through a flashback in which he recalls tearfully a Mafia-style massacre at his wedding to Gloriana. There is a terrifying Punch-and-Judy sequence as he talks to the skull. Eddie Izzard plays a metrosexual Lussurioso: vain, petty and all-powerful (see photo on page 170). Derek Jacobi plays the Duke as impenetrable and supremely powerful, with a pronounced weakness for illicit sex. The play is heavily amended, but through the headlong pace and the black humour, the insecurity and hopelessness of individuals are strongly evident. It achieves a clear insight into the text and how its first audiences might have responded.

2004 Stewart McGill, directing the Playbox Theatre at the Dream Factory, Warwick – perhaps because there were more women than men in the company – switched some of the characters' genders. There was loud music and a mood of cool, sinister confidence.

2004 Jamie Harper at the London Academy of Music and Dramatic Art opted for a more traditional approach, using elaborate Jacobean costumes, but opened by staging the rape of Antonio's wife, surrounded by masked men. He cast females as Ambitioso and Supervacuo, perhaps echoing the wicked sisters Goneril and Regan in Shakespeare's *King Lear*.

2008 Melly Still's production at the National Theatre reflected her idea that Middleton was satirizing the sexist views of a corrupt patriarchal society, where the only route to justice and redemption was through a virtuous woman. Rory Kinnear played Vindice as half-maddened by the vices of his society and half-philosophical, perhaps in a nod towards Hamlet. Hence he seemed to lose himself in his violent cruelty, but recovered and died stoically, almost with relief. The play opened with a rape scene and closed with the tearful responses of mother and sister to the news of the execution of Vindice and Hippolito. The human cost, particularly to women, of the immorality and cruelty of the corrupt regime was made clear.

2008   At the Royal Exchange Theatre, Manchester, directed by Jonathan Moore, Vindice was played by Stephen Tompkinson (see photo below). The play was presented in starker, less complex terms, with summary justice dispensed either by poison or the sword in a violent, bloodthirsty production.

Stephen Tompkinson as Vindice in the Royal Exchange Theatre production, 2008

There is usually a current production of *The Revenger's Tragedy* somewhere in the UK; for example in 2009 it was performed at the Studio Theatre, Arts Institute, Bournemouth; in 2010 at the Rose Theatre, Kingston, with Director Emeritus, Sir Peter Hall; and in 2011 by the amateur company at the Edward Alderton Theatre, Bexleyheath, Kent. If you search through the press and the Internet you are likely to discover a production that you could attend.

Critical views

Thomas Middleton's plays were well-regarded and successful, culminating in the popularity of *A Game at Chess*, which marked both the height of Middleton's career and the start of his decline. The play was banned by the censors, who seem to have shunned most of the author's later work (see page 6).

Unlike Ben Jonson, who issued a folio edition of his collected works in 1616, and Shakespeare, with the First Folio edition of his works appearing in 1623, neither Middleton nor any of his colleagues collected his writing. It remained scattered in the hands of individuals. Compounding this problem was the inaccurate recording of the authorship of works such as *The Revenger's Tragedy*, and other failures in attributing to him works he had written or co-written. As a result, there was little contemporary commentary upon Middleton's body of work. However, his dramas influenced later playwrights such as Philip Massinger and James Shirley in the 1620s and 1630s.

It is generally agreed that the revenge drama tradition ended with John Ford's *'Tis Pity She's a Whore*, performed between 1629 and 1633; its presentation of incest and the sympathy shown to the incestuous protagonists drew much criticism. In 1642 the theatres were closed by the Puritan government, reopening 18 years later after the restoration of Charles II to the throne. With the restoration, a new form of comic drama became fashionable and Middleton's plays disappeared from the stage for many years.

Generally, critics of the nineteenth century were shocked and repelled by *The Revenger's Tragedy*. John Churton Collins viewed Middleton as a writer whose art was ruined by his fixation with sin, lust and wretchedness; he believed that minor characters 'lacked colour' and that Middleton's vision was too narrow. John Addington Symonds saw Vindice as a 'scorpion of revenge' and a 'moral leper' in a 'crooked play'; however, he admired the characterization of the protagonist.

In the early twentieth century, William Archer regarded the play as a 'monstrous melodrama' that should not be taken seriously. Although T.S. Eliot considered that the horror and loathing that he felt governed the play expressed the author's own view of life, he admired the highly poetic skills of such an 'isolated masterpiece'.

Modern critics have gone much further in assessing the greatness of Middleton's achievement, and there is a wide range of critical comment (for the work done to identify Middleton as the author of the play, see pages 2–3). Critics studying *The Revenger's Tragedy* have worked in the following areas:

- the biography of Middleton
- humanist criticism and issues of morality
- questions of genre
- cultural materialist criticism
- the contexts of the play
- the theatricality of the play
- issues of women and gender.

See Further Reading, pages 232–234, for publication details of all the works mentioned below.

Biography

Relatively little is known about Thomas Middleton's life, and it is neatly presented in *Thomas Middleton: The Collected Works*, edited by Gary Taylor and John Lavagnino. This provides a wealth of interesting biographical and contextual detail ranging through his life, society in the City of London, and the theatres of his time.

Earlier brief studies were written by Mark Eccles in 'Middleton's Birth and Education' (*Review of English Studies*, 1931), and 'Thomas Middleton a Poett' (*Studies in Philology*, 1957).

Humanism and morality

Much early twentieth-century criticism was humanist, concerned for the condition of humankind within the universe. The concept of the tragic hero embraced the idea of the individual who suffers and dies for the sake of others, or for justice. There have always been critics concerned with Middleton's views on morality. Robert Ornstein, in *The Moral Vision of Jacobean Tragedy*, argues that Middleton presents a coherent moral framework that controls the orderly structure of *The Revenger's Tragedy*. In *Renaissance Revivals: City Comedy and Revenge Tragedy in the London Theatre, 1576–1980*, Wendy Griswold suggests that revenge plays are concerned with moral, social and political issues and, despite problems such as those created by the court of James I, end with a restoration of state order. M.C. Bradbrook's *Themes and Conventions of Elizabethan Tragedy* considers 22 'ironic reversals' that help determine the structure of the play.

Genre

Many critics have discussed the genre of this play; perhaps one of the most influential is Nicholas Brooke in *Horrid Laughter in Jacobean Tragedy*. Brooke argues that a stylized combination of laughter and horror creates a sense simultaneously of order and of frantic, barely controlled disorder. Peter Mercer, in *Hamlet and the Acting of Revenge*, explores the influences upon *The Revenger's Tragedy* of Seneca and John Marston, arguing that Middleton's sense of outrage at the social corruption led by the court prompted his ideas. Claiming that the author was anxious about sexuality, Mercer writes that Vindice, little more than a mocking entertainer, is not suited as the protagonist of tragedy. Robert N. Watson explores *The Revenger's Tragedy* in the wider context of Elizabethan and Jacobean tragedy in his essay 'Tragedy' in *The*

Cambridge Companion to English Renaissance Drama, edited by A.R. Braunmuller and Michael Hattaway. Other critics address debts to writers of tragedies such as Thomas Kyd and Shakespeare, and trace the influence of the earlier morality genre upon Middleton's work.

Cultural materialism

'Cultural materialist' critics address the play within the specific socio-political context of its age. J.W. Lever, in *The Tragedy of State*, offers a very accessible study of a play set at the time when the certainties and security of the feudal system were being torn apart by a new capitalism, which left many people of the middle and lower classes adrift and poorer. Jonathan Dollimore builds upon this argument in *Radical Tragedy*. His criticism moves into the area known as 'new historicism', since he re-assesses the play within its broader historical context. He argues that Middleton boldly confronts a critical breakdown in the traditional social order, one that undermines the idea of a providential divine scheme of salvation for humankind; Middleton reveals the secrecy of the power structure and social control at the court of James I. There is a more general account of the play's cultural contexts in Swapan Chakravorty's *Society and Politics in the Plays of Thomas Middleton*.

Context

Two modern authors go on to further contextualize the play for students. In *Shakespeare and Renaissance Drama*, Hugh Mackay includes a section on Jacobean revenge drama, with specific references to Middleton's ideas on sexuality, disguise, morality, misogyny, the use of the supernatural and the role of women. Similarly Michelle O'Callaghan, in *Thomas Middleton: Renaissance Dramatist*, includes a wide range of contexts – biographical, historical, poetical and cultural. In another accessible study, *The*

Revenger's Madness: A Study of Revenge Tragedy Motifs, Charles A. Hallett and Elaine S. Hallett place revenge tragedy within its social and political contexts, arguing its relevance to a broken society.

Theatricality

Middleton is a master of stagecraft, and there are some highly engaging discussions about the theatricality of *The Revenger's Tragedy*. The liveliest account of the play in performance is that by Stanley Wells ('*The Revenger's Tragedy* Revived', in *The Elizabethan Theatre 6*, ed. George Hibbard) of the triumphant RSC production which ended at the Aldwych Theatre in 1969. Howard Felperin, in *Shakespearean Representation*, claims that the theatricality of the play undermines its moral argument. Scott McMillin argues against this in 'Acting and Violence: *The Revenger's Tragedy* and its Departures from *Hamlet*' (*Studies in English Literature*, 1984). Instead, McMillin claims the theatricality and role-playing are related to the issue of identity.

Gender issues

Since the last quarter of the twentieth century, critics have addressed topics that used to be called 'feminist', but which are now given the truer and wider title of 'gender' issues. Among these, Catherine Belsey, in *The Subject of Tragedy*, argues that there is a sophisticated conceptualization of gender in the play, which creates a radical approach to identity and meaning. Peter Stallybrass, in 'Reading the Body: *The Revenger's Tragedy* and the Jacobean Theatre of Consumption' (*Renaissance Drama*, 1987), discusses the function of women in the play.

The Revenger's Tragedy has appealed to audiences for over 400 years. The issues it raises and the ways in which it presents them seem as relevant today as any contemporary black comedy. This striking and thought-provoking drama seems destined to continue to fascinate and challenge audiences.

Essay Questions

1 How does Middleton present his ideas about justice in *The Revenger's Tragedy*?

2 Explore the ways in which Middleton uses imagery of gold and jewellery in *The Revenger's Tragedy*.

3 To what extent is Vindice a victim of his society?

4 Critics suggest that money is a central issue in this play. How far do you agree, and how does Middleton present this idea?

5 Discuss Middleton's use of humour in *The Revenger's Tragedy*, and the effects he creates.

6 Consider how Middleton uses the illegitimate Spurio in developing his ideas in the play.

7 Is Middleton more interested in presenting devils than saints in *The Revenger's Tragedy*?

8 Explore the first scene as an opening to the play.

9 Why is sex and sexuality so important in *The Revenger's Tragedy*?

10 Why does Middleton present so many revengers and revenges in his play?

11 Explore your response to Antonio and the ways in which he is presented in the play.

12 Is there any optimism in the ending of *The Revenger's Tragedy*?

13 How might Middleton offer a warning to today's society through *The Revenger's Tragedy*?

14 Is Hippolito simply Vindice's junior apprentice? Explore the ways in which Middleton presents this character.

15 Critics agree that Middleton likes to shock his audience. Discuss the ways in which he creates shocking effects, and their significance in the play.

16 Explore Middleton's stagecraft and the theatricality of *The Revenger's Tragedy*.

17 Has religion any relevance in the world of this play? Discuss the ways that it is represented in Middleton's imagery.

18 Is *The Revenger's Tragedy* really a tragedy? Discuss your ideas on the genre of the play.

19 How dangerous is Lussurioso? Consider how Middleton presents him.

20 Explore the effectiveness of Middleton's use of language by closely examining two or three passages in the play.

21 In what ways is *The Revenger's Tragedy* still relevant to society today?

22 Is *The Revenger's Tragedy* a misogynistic play? Discuss the ways in which it presents women.

23 Discuss the suggestion that the virtuous characters carry little weight in the audience's response to the play.

24 Is Vindice hopelessly entrapped in the corrupt world he describes so eloquently?

Chronology

Thomas Middleton's life

1568   William Middleton, Thomas's father, granted a coat of arms.

1574   William Middleton marries his second wife, Anne.

1580   Thomas Middleton born in London.

1582   His sister Avis born.

1586   William Middleton dies; Anne Middleton marries Thomas Harvey.

1597   Middleton writes *Wisdom of Solomon Paraphrased*.

1598   Middleton goes up to Queen's College, Oxford; his sister Avis marries Allan Waterer.

1599   Middleton's poem *The Ghost of Lucrece* published.

1600/1601   Middleton leaves Oxford.

1601   Middleton receives £25 from the City of London Orphan's fund; in London he accompanies the players.

1602   Middleton receives his first payment for a play, a collaboration on *Caesar's Fall* (lost).

c. 1603   Marries Mary Magdalen Marbeck.

1604   Middleton collaborates on 'The Magnificent Entertainment', a pageant celebrating the accession of James I for the City of London; *The Phoenix*, his comedy, performed at court and at St Paul's Theatre; his comedy *The Honest Whore* acted by Prince Henry's Men at the Fortune Theatre.

1605   Writes the city comedies *A Trick to Catch the Old One* and *A Mad World, My Masters*.

1606   Writes *The Revenger's Tragedy*.

1609   Middleton moves with his wife Mary to his permanent home at Newington, Surrey.

1611   Middleton writes *The Roaring Girl*, with Thomas Dekker.

1613 His city comedy *A Chaste Maid in Cheapside* performed; Middleton writes and produces the first of his many civic pageants.

1618 James I authorizes a special patent for publication of Middleton's *The Peace-Maker*, a treatise condemning violence.

1620 Middleton is granted an annual salary by the City of London for recording contemporary London life for posterity.

1621 Middleton's *Women Beware Women* acted.

1622 Middleton's *The Changeling*, with William Rowley, acted.

1624 Middleton's *A Game at Chess* acted, but subsequently banned by censors; this signals the end of his career.

1627 Thomas Middleton dies.

1628 His widow dies in poverty.

Historical, literary and cultural events

1558 Mary I dies; accession of Elizabeth I.

1564 Christopher Marlowe, William Shakespeare born.

1572 Thomas Dekker, Ben Jonson born.

1575 John Marston, Cyril Tourneur born.

1576 'The Theatre' built, the first in London.

c. 1580 John Webster born.

1586 John Ford born.

c. 1587 Thomas Kyd's *The Spanish Tragedy* acted; the Rose Theatre opens.

1588 Spanish Armada defeated.

1588/1592 Marlowe's *Dr Faustus* acted.

1590 High prices cause economic depression, especially rurally.

1599 Globe Theatre opens; satires proscribed and burnt.

c. 1601 Shakespeare's *Hamlet* acted.

1603 Elizabeth I dies; accession of James I (James VI of Scotland); Chamberlain's Men become the King's Men.

1604 Marston's *The Malcontent* acted.

1605 The Gunpowder Plot; George Chapman, Ben Jonson and John Marston imprisoned when their satire *Eastward Ho!* offends James I.

1606 Jonson's *Volpone* acted.

1608 The King's Men established at Blackfriars Theatre.

1611 The Authorized Version of the Bible (King James Bible) published.

1613 Globe Theatre burns down.

1623 'First Folio' of Shakespeare's works published.

1625 James I dies; accession of Charles I.

1629 Charles I dissolves Parliament and decides to govern without it.

1629/1633 Ford's *Tis Pity She's a Whore* acted.

1642 Civil war; the closing of the theatres.

1649 Charles I executed; Commonwealth.

1660 Restoration of Charles II; theatres reopen.

Further Reading

Biography of Thomas Middleton

Mark Eccles, 'Middleton's Birth and Education', *Review of English Studies* 7, 1931, pp. 431–441

Mark Eccles, 'Thomas Middleton a Poett', *Studies in Philology* 54, 1957, pp. 516–536

Gary Taylor and John Lavagnino (eds), *Thomas Middleton: The Collected Works* (Oxford University Press, 2007)

Sources for *The Revenger's Tragedy*

N.W. Bawcutt, '*The Revenger's Tragedy* and the Medici Family', *Notes and Queries*, May 1957

N.W. Bawcutt, 'The Assassination of Alessandro de'Medici in Early Seventeenth-Century English Drama', *Review of English Studies* 56, 2005, pp. 412–423

G.K Hunter, 'A Source for *The Revenger's Tragedy*', *Review of English Studies* 10, 1959, pp. 181–182

Authorship of *The Revenger's Tragedy*

R.V. Holdsworth (ed.), *Three Jacobean Revenge Tragedies*, Casebook Series (Palgrave Macmillan, 1990)

MacDonald P. Jackson, *Studies in Attribution: Middleton and Shakespeare* (University of Salzburg, 1979)

David J. Lake, *The Canon of Thomas Middleton's Plays: Internal Evidence for the Major Problems of Authorship* (Cambridge University Press, 1975)

Critical books and articles

Catherine Belsey, *The Subject of Tragedy: Identity and Difference in Renaissance Drama* (Methuen/Routledge, 1985)

M.C. Bradbrook, *Themes and Conventions of Elizabethan Tragedy* (Cambridge University Press, 1935)

A.R. Braunmuller and Michael Hattaway (eds), *The Cambridge Companion to English Renaissance Drama* (Cambridge University Press, 1990)

Nicholas Brooke, *Horrid Laughter in Jacobean Tragedy* (Open Books, 1979)

Swapan Chakravorty, *Society and Politics in the Plays of Thomas Middleton* (Clarendon Press, 1996)

Jonathan Dollimore, *Radical Tragedy: Religion, Ideology and Power in the Drama of Shakespeare and his Contemporaries* (Prentice Hall, 1984)

Howard Felperin, *Shakespearean Representation* (Princeton University Press, 1977)

Roma Gill, 'The World of Thomas Middleton', in *Accompaninge the Players: Essays Celebrating Thomas Middleton 1580–1980*, ed. Kenneth Friedenreich (AMS Press, 1983)

Wendy Griswold, *Renaissance Revivals: City Comedy and Revenge Tragedy in the London Theatre, 1576–1980* (University of Chicago Press, 1986)

Charles A. Hallett and Elaine S. Hallett, *The Revenger's Madness: A Study of Revenge Tragedy Motifs* (University of Nebraska Press, 1980)

R.V. Holdsworth (ed.), *Three Jacobean Revenge Tragedies*, Casebook Series (Palgrave Macmillan, 1990)

J.W. Lever, *The Tragedy of State* (Methuen, 1971)

Hugh Mackay, *Shakespeare and Renaissance Drama* (Longman, 2010)

Scott McMillin, 'Acting and Violence: *The Revenger's Tragedy* and its Departures from *Hamlet*', *Studies in English Literature* Vol. 24 No. 2 (Spring 1984), pp. 275–291

Peter Mercer, *Hamlet and the Acting of Revenge* (Palgrave Macmillan, 1987)

Michelle O'Callaghan, *Thomas Middleton: Renaissance Dramatist* (Edinburgh University Press, 2009)

Robert Ornstein, *The Moral Vision of Jacobean Tragedy* (Greenwood Press, 1960)

Peter Stallybrass, 'Reading the Body: *The Revenger's Tragedy* and the Jacobean Theatre of Consumption', *Renaissance Drama* 18, 1987, pp. 121–148

Stanley Wells, '*The Revenger's Tragedy* Revived', in *The Elizabethan Theatre* 6, ed. George Hibbard (University of Waterloo, 1978)

DVDs

Revengers Tragedy directed by Alex Cox (Fantoma Films, 2002)

Archive video of Di Trevis's 1987 production at the Royal Shakespeare Theatre is available at the Shakespeare Centre Library and Archive, library@shakespeare.org.uk, reference RSC/TS/2/2/1987/REV1

Websites

For further critical perspectives on performances and productions, see the websites of individual theatres or actors. To find Middleton criticism online, use a search engine such as Google.